REAL COOL
COLORADO PLACES
FOR CURIOUS KIDS

Text and Photography by
Diane T. Liggett and James A. Mack

WESTCLIFFE PUBLISHERS

Englewood, Colorado

ISBN: 1-56579-293-9

The graphic on page 118 is printed with permission from the book *Tracking Dinosaurs: A New Look at an Ancient World*, by Martin Lockley, copyright 1991 University of Colorado and Cambridge University Press.

Editor: Sallie Greenwood
Designer: Mark Mulvany & Tim George
Map Designer: Jonathan Moreno
Production Manager: Harlene Finn

Published by: Westcliffe Publishers, Inc.
P.O. Box 1261
Englewood, Colorado 80150

Printed in: Hong Kong through World Print Ltd.

Library of Congress Cataloging-in-Publication Data:

Liggett, Diane T., 1960–
        Real cool Colorado places for curious kids / text and photography
    by Diane T. Liggett and James A. Mack.
            p. cm.
        Includes bibliographical references.
        ISBN 1-56579-293-9
        1. Colorado—Guidebooks. 2. Family recreation—Colorado–
    –Guidebooks 3. Children—Travel—Colorado—Guidebooks. I. Mack,
    James A., 1944– . II. Title.
    F774.3.L54 1998
    917.8804'33—dc21

                                                                    97-48551
                                                                        CIP

For more information about other fine books and calendars from Westcliffe Publishers, please call your local bookstore, contact us at 1-800-523-3692, or write for our free color catalog.

Cover captions: (Clockwise from top left:) Rocky Mountain National Park (National Park Service), Mesa Verde National Park, Creede, and Great Sand Dunes National Monument.

Acknowledgments

Capturing the essence of Colorado's coolest places in writing and on 35mm film was an enjoyable challenge made easier with generous assistance from certain individuals and organizations.

Special thanks goes to Grand Junction teacher and devoted Bureau of Land Management volunteer Marty Felix (a.k.a. the Bookcliff Wild Horse Lady) for sharing her photographs and stories of the wild mustangs; sculptor Madeline Wiener, program director for the Marble Institute of Colorado; Capt. Laurel E. Scherer and the cadet falconers of the U.S. Air Force Academy; Creede Repertory Theatre, San Juan Sports of Creede, and the tour guides at Creede's fine Underground Mining Museum; First American Railways and Amos Cordova, vice president, Durango & Silverton Narrow Gauge Railroad; Deborah Muehleisen, director of marketing, Royal Gorge Bridge; Denver Museum of Natural History; Vickie Pierce, manager of administration and outreach for the Colorado Geological Survey; Kathy Brown, chief of interpretation, Great Sand Dunes National Monument; Maggie Johnston, chief ranger, Florissant Fossil Beds National Monument; Colorado Department of Transportation; Clint McKnight, publications specialist for the Dinosaur Nature Association; and the historic Bross Hotel in Paonia.

Also especially helpful was Barbara Day of the Colorado Historical Society in researching historic photographs. And finally, of particular importance, was the enthusiastic response about this project from parents and teachers, who provided great encouragement along the way.

There are more awesome places for kids to explore in Colorado than you can count. From wilderness trails guarded by colossal stone sentinels here in Rocky Mountain National Park, to surprising sites near cities, extraordinary opportunities await the most inquisitive adventurers. So crank up your sense of curiosity and let your imagination run wild as you visit these outstanding Colorado destinations.

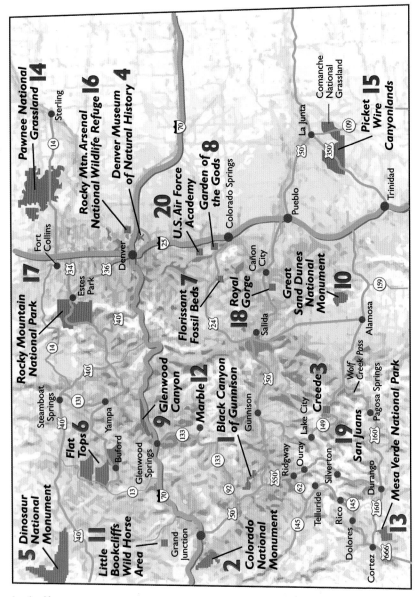

Jonathan Moreno

Contents

Introduction

The world is saturated with artificial places and thrills. Receding into the edges of our lives are the real places and experiences—no artificial flavors or colors added. This book is about discovering the coolest authentic places in Colorado and learning the most intriguing things about them. Each chapter lets you respond to your own interests and encounter ideas and experiences that will last longer than any memories gained from ordinary entertainment.

This is a family guide, centered around interests in real, one-of-a-kind destinations. Without a doubt, Colorado's diverse geography and equally varied range of human and prehistoric history provide unlimited opportunities to learn, explore, and adventure. As a result, the real cool places are scattered around the state—near and far from population centers. Many nearby destinations reveal surprising stories. Some far-flung sites echo with the sounds of the past, whether from a miner's pickax or the ponderous shuffle of dinosaurs, the essential ingredients for an unforgettable experience are your imagination, your curiosity, and your sense of adventure.

Diane T. Liggett & James A. Mack

Colorado's real cool places take kids of all ages down paths of adventure and learning. From well-known natural sites such as Rocky Mountain National Park, pictured here, to more remote destinations in the state, Colorado offers memorable experiences for everyone. Curiosity is an essential ingredient to enjoy a fascinating excursion so take it with you wherever you go. National Park Service

Definition of Symbols

Discovery Zone

Each real cool place in Colorado is a discovery zone for amazing facts, fun, excitement, and astonishment. In this section, you'll find out about the most interesting things to see and do in the state. Everything is included from a visit to the plains of Africa at the Denver Museum of Natural History to a jump off a 700-foot-high sand dune at Great Sand Dunes National Monument.

Paleo Scene

Colorado is rich in fossil discoveries and ancient secrets in stone. Here you'll find out about places where paleontology is the main attraction. At Picket Wire Canyonlands, you can walk along one of the largest dinosaur trackways in North America. You'll find a petrified tree stump as big as your garage at Florissant Fossil Beds National Monument. Visit one of these prehistoric destinations that once weren't cool at all!

Crypto Scene

There is no way to know all the secrets of Colorado's cool places. Almost every destination offers some cryptic or hidden puzzles to solve. This section reveals little-known stories such as behind the scenes at the Denver Museum of Natural History where trees, flowers, and dinosaurs are made. With a few clues, you may even unravel the mystery of a disappearing river at Great Sand Dunes National Monument!

Wild Things

From galloping stallions to bighorn rams, this state is one of the wildest places around. Here you'll encounter wildlife from almost every corner of Colorado. Once you meet the mustangs of the Little Bookcliffs or the bugling elk of Rocky Mountain National Park, you will always hear the call of the wild in Colorado.

Micro Scape

A world of wonder sometimes rests right at your feet or just beyond your direct line of sight. Take a look at, under, and into some of the smallest or unique things in Colorado. Visit the Flat Tops and find out why aspens quake, and learn how prairie plants survive howling winds at Pawnee National Grassland. Keep your eyes and ears open wherever you go. There's more to Colorado than meets the eye.

Back in Time Line

Imagine walking on a path traveled thousands of years ago by people who later vanished! This section reveals the colorful history of Colorado from the cliff dwellings of Mesa Verde National Park to a narrow-gauge railroad in the San Juan Mountains. You'll become a time traveler once you get a taste of the state's fascinating past.

Travel Log

Here you will find the most important information for enjoying your excursions. Directions, addresses, campground locations, and safety precautions will help you and your family gear up for a successful adventure. Colorado's real cool places are just waiting for you, so find a good area map before you hit the road and get ready to encounter the unexpected!

Black Canyon of the Gunnison

Discovery Zone

"Oh-my-gosh!"

"Wow!"

Other visitors are speechless at the sight of the Black Canyon's precipitous gorge. Breathtaking, to say the least, Black Canyon's granite walls plunge more than a thousand feet to the Gunnison River. The dizzying distance from top to bottom makes you wonder if the muffled sound you hear is the river far below, the wind, or your heart as you steady yourself against the sturdy railing at The Narrows View overlook.

Deep, Dark, and Difficult

Why is it called Black Canyon? At The Narrows View overlook, 1,300 feet separate you from the slightly higher rim to the south; the gorge is deeper at this point than it is wide. At Painted Wall, its deepest point, the top soars 2,300 feet above the river. These depths and narrowness barely allow the sun to reach the Gunnison, thus the name Black Canyon.

Peering into the dark canyon is the main attraction here, and there are overlooks on the north and south rims that provide dramatic vistas. Some visitors cannot resist the challenge of scrambling into the intimidating gulch just because it's there. If you are tempted to explore, you should know that early visitors pronounced the canyon impassable. There are no marked trails into the canyon so careful preparation is critical. Even the hardiest outdoors person is challenged by the daunting hike into the canyon.

Part of the monument is designated wilderness, an inviting backcountry experience. You'll need a permit, and it's advisable to talk with a park ranger for route information and conditions. You must be prepared, too, for self-rescue. As with any wilderness adventure, you enter the area on its terms, and you must be self-sufficient. You should be in good to excellent physical condition; distances can be deceiving. Descent times to the river range from 1.5 to 2.5 hours, doubling or tripling for the climb out. One reward for the trip is the opportunity to fish for trophy-size trout in one of Colorado's eleven gold medal streams.

Camping is another good reason to visit Black Canyon of the Gunnison. The campgrounds, one on each rim, offer pleasant and relaxing experiences. Dirt roads on the north rim provide easy mountain biking access to overlooks.

The Black Canyon of the Gunnison is known for its dark and mysterious grandeur, its thrilling depths, and its natural splendor.

From its headwaters in the mountains to the east, the Gunnison River flows westward, to join the Colorado River at Grand Junction. Millions of years ago, the Gunnison established its original course through terrain of basalt or volcanic rock. Gradually the landscape started to rise, like a giant bubble, into a dome. Determined to maintain its course as the land rose, the river continued to cut through the basalt like a knife through a layer cake. Such downward cutting soon reached a layer of metamorphic rock, called gneiss (NICE). Metamorphic comes from the Greek words *meta*, meaning change, and *morph*, meaning form. Intense heat and pressures underground virtually changed the form and structure of the original, or parent, rock. Black Canyon gneiss, sometimes called basement rock, is nearly 2 billion years old, and it is also found in the Grand Canyon.

The gneiss was subjected to further changes much later, when molten granite was forced upward and squeezed like toothpaste from a tube into crevices in the gneiss. This created jagged white and pink veins or streaks, called intrusions, in the rocks, and the contrasting color of the intrusive granite makes the canyon walls look as though they had been painted, thus the name Painted Wall. One of the most outstanding features of the monument, this rock face is a picturesque result of geologic forces. Painted Wall, at 2,300 feet high, is Colorado's highest cliff.

Wild Things

Bird-watching is great at Black Canyon because habitats vary from streamsides to scrub oak woodlands and offer plenty of water, food, and protection. Along *Chasm View Nature Trail* you can watch violet-green swallows and white-throated swifts dip over the canyon walls to catch insects in midflight.

You might see a vivid orange and yellow western tanager or a rufous-sided towhee brighten the piñon and juniper woodlands along the rim. Blue grouse and peregrine falcons are more difficult to see because of their elusive behavior and small populations. *Warner Point Nature Trail* on the south rim is a good spot to begin your lifelong hobby of bird-watching, so strap on some binoculars and start your birding checklist at Black Canyon.

Micro Scape

Although the jagged rocks of Black Canyon appear dark and forbidding, close examination reveals a colorful world of tiny organisms. Spreading out over the rocks in patches of white, orange, bright green, and gray, lichens perform a significant role in nature.

Like tiny gardens, delicate and colorful combinations of fungus and algae cover rock surfaces. Each partner plant in this symbiotic relationship contributes to the survival of the other.

Lichens, a combination of fungus and algae living together, secrete an acid that breaks down hard rock. Although this process takes many years, solid stone eventually crumbles from the action of these organisms. Why is this important? Lichens create smaller pieces of rock that eventually form soil. Plant seeds drop onto these new, shallow soils and may sprout and turn into tough vegetation that provides food and shelter for wildlife.

Back in Time Line

Wallace Hansen, a geologist who studied the area, noted that other western canyons may be larger, deeper, and narrower, "But no other canyon in North America combines the depth, narrowness, sheerness, and somber countenance of the Black Canyon of the Gunnison."

Early explorers, including Capt. John W. Gunnison, for whom the river was named, avoided the canyon when he was surveying the area for a transcontinental railroad route in 1853. He wasn't the only one to find the steep walls and narrow canyon intimidating though. Even Ute Indians avoided it.

The first Europeans to explore the canyon were with Ferdinand V. Hayden in 1873–1874. Hayden, leader of a government survey of western lands, documented the wonders of the Yellowstone area in 1871. When the survey's notes, sketches, and photographs reached eastern cities, they provided dramatic

The river below Painted Wall threads its way over and around boulders that have crashed down from the canyon walls. Descending the steep slopes to the river is a definite challenge. L. Lynch, National Park Service

glimpses of the geothermal features and other spectacular sights of the Yellowstone Valley. Hayden surveyed much of the west and recorded his observations and collected rock specimens.

Indians called him Man Who Picks Up Stones Running because he traveled quickly and wanted to collect as much information as possible in a short time. Imagine what his thoughts would be today, when we examine lunar rock samples and anticipate the day when robotic space explorers bring back rocks from Mars!

The unknown has always driven people with a sense of adventure and curiosity to investigate unfamiliar places and defy amazing odds. Abraham Lincoln Fellows heard that the Black Canyon was "impassable," but decided to take the risk, despite obvious dangers. He had a professional motive, too, because he was to survey the canyon for a possible water diversion tunnel to be built by the state of Colorado.

He and a partner, William Torrence, spent nine days in the canyon in 1901. Fellows noted in his journal that when he and Torrence reached the point where no other explorer had dared on the river, that he had "the feeling of nervousness and dread." His concern was for his partner, and he warned Torrence, "if we cross the river at this point there can be no return . . . I do not ask you to go, but leave the decision entirely to yourself. As for me, I am going through."

And they did go through the canyon and proved the canyon was passable, but not without many harrowing obstacles and life-threatening moments. They each lost 15 pounds and suffered bruises and scrapes against the sharp rocks in the Gunnison's swift current. Their reward came eight years later when the six-mile-long Gunnison Diversion Tunnel was completed and started carrying water to irrigate nearby farms.

Travel Log

• The north rim of the Black Canyon of the Gunnison offers fewer services than the south rim but makes up for it by providing more spectacular views of the canyon. The north rim road is closed in winter. In summer, access to the north rim is from Colorado 92, near Crawford.

• The south rim is easily reached on Colorado 347, just east of Montrose on U.S. 50. South rim roads are paved and a visitor center has geology, flora and fauna, and local history exhibits. Both sides of the canyon have first-come, first-served campgrounds that charge a fee. Water is in very limited supply and must be trucked in. You need to bring your own firewood and charcoal.

Wayside exhibits at canyon overlooks provide the opportunity to understand the geology and human history of the area. Visitors spend time studying the signs to help make their vacations more informative. L. Lynch, National Park Service

2
Colorado National Monument

If the sandstone walls at Colorado National Monument could talk, they might whisper of events no humans recall. Soaring 300 feet above the Grand Valley floor, tawny cliffs would tell of windstorms when sand dunes covered this area of Colorado. Naturally sculpted into towering works of art, the deep orange or rust Entrada Formations would reflect on millions of years of erosion. Disconnected from the lowlands near the Colorado River, the bleached rocks of the Morrison Formation would describe Jurassic events when dinosaurs tromped the earth.

A thousand years ago, Fremont Indians considered the walls of Monument, Wedding, Ute, and Red Canyons as canvas for their petroglyphs. Utes followed, leading their ponies to pastures in Glade Park.

Visitors enjoy producing astounding echoes at monument overlooks.

Rim Rock Drive cuts through cliffs of Wingate sandstone near the monument's west entrance. Snaking steeply from the Grand Valley below, this unforgettable road gains almost 2,000 feet in elevation.

In 1911, these towering cliffs became Colorado National Monument. Today visitors linger at Ute Canyon View or Cold Shivers Point to listen to echoes. These walls can really talk back! Messages ricochet over and over again. As you enjoy the panoramic views along Rim Rock Drive, check out the echoes at other overlooks. Some bounce back, while others just whistle with the wind.

Paleo Scene

Identifying exposed rock formations presents a challenging exercise while traveling up Rim Rock Drive. Amateur geologists must be quick and observant to detect passing chapters in the unfolding story of Colorado National Monument.

After you enter the monument, rocks quickly shift from sandy-hued, dinosaur-age (more than 200 million years ago) Morrison shale to dark gray gneiss, schist, and granite more than 600 million years old. This Precambrian crossing marks an ancient fault line where the younger rocks of Colorado National Monument were forced 2,000 feet above the valley floor. Some of these layers of buff-colored rock actually bend over at the northern edge of the Uncompahgre Plateau where the fault occurred.

At the base of the monument cliffs rests the Chinle Formation, deep red sandstone and shale deposited by floods and desert winds. The perpendicular walls of Wingate sandstone come next, also etched by winds and floods.

Look for the intricate crossbedding that indicates fossilized dunes in these Triassic cliffs. Topped off by the hard ledges of the Kayenta Formation, great golden walls give way to rust-colored Entrada sandstone that forms the most interesting sculptures in the monument.

The Morrison and Dakota Formations reappear in the highest portions of Colorado National Monument. Once forming caprock that protected the Entrada ridges, most of these younger rocks have washed away, leaving the Entrada to battle the elements on its own.

What Makes a Monument?

Look at Independence Monument and try to connect it with the Entrada sandstone ridges to the north and south. An immense rock wall like this once separated Monument and Wedding Canyons. As rain and wind broadened the canyons, the wall narrowed, surrendering to erosion. Where natural fractures further weakened the ridge, parts of it collapsed, leaving expansive holes. Independence Monument, 450-feet high, was isolated, still protected by stubborn Kayenta caprock.

Descend Through Time

Numerous trails offer visitors a closer look at the monument's sandstone sculptures. Most of the short walks to the rim are easy and present great photo opportunities. Backcountry trails are more challenging, though. Remember, what goes down must come up, so save plenty of water and energy to trudge back to the trailhead.

• *Monument Canyon Trail*—Save most of a day for the trip down this 6-mile (one-way) trail. Even if you only hike part way, you will want to take your time. While you make the very steep 600-foot descent past Coke Ovens on the right, you can test your knowledge of time by examining the distinct rock layers. The trail winds around on red Chinle soil past huge rust-colored

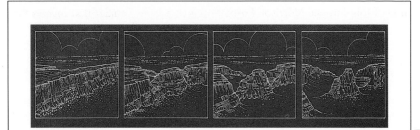

Sandstone sculptures, such as Independence Monument, began as solid rock walls. Over time, erosion widened canyons causing the walls to narrow and weaken. Weathering along fractures made the stone crumble, leaving gaps and creating free-standing monoliths. National Park Service

The distinct impression of a Diplodocus *leg-bone lures hikers to the* Dinosaur Hill Trail *just outside the west entrance to the monument. Numerous outstanding fossil sites in this part of western Colorado and eastern Utah make up the "Dinosaur Triangle," where visitors can experience more pieces of the region's prehistoric past.*

alcoves of Entrada sandstone. Beyond Cleopatra's Couch and the Kissing Couple, Independence Monument steals the show.

•   *Window Rock Trail*—If you spend the night at Saddlehorn Campground, rise early and take the short hike toward the edge of Wedding Canyon. You will never forget the first shafts of light reaching the mesa tops. This is also a good time to see birds of prey cruise above the canyon rim.

•   *Dinosaur Hill Trail*—Dinosaur fossils have been discovered just outside the monument's west entrance, on Colorado 340. The first stop on the short trail of this Jurassic Morrison Formation is at a large boulder that reveals the huge impression of a *Diplodocus* femur. The rest of the walking tour is, of course, history!

Crypto Scene

Rattlesnake Canyon, just west of the monument, is for serious explorers. Despite its name, snakes are not the main attraction at this Bureau of Land Management Wilderness Study Area beyond Black Ridge. It is rock formations that draw adventurous visitors.

Here is the world's second largest concentration of natural arches, after Arches National Park in Utah. At least nine arches, ranging from a modest circular skylight in a paper-thin dome to a span 120 feet high and 80 feet wide, have been weathered from the sandstone ridge by water and wind.

Rattlesnake Arches was formed from years of gravel grinding away at potholes in Entrada sandstone. Water seeping through these openings, along with wind-blown sand, continues to weather the enormous alcoves below.

It is thrilling to walk along the trail that skirts the top of these arches. Views are 100 feet straight down through openings created by years of water and gravel abrading the bottoms of potholes; over time, water falling into the alcoves combined with wind-blown sand to shape the graceful arches.

Exploring the arches from the wooded shelf below is unforgettable, especially if you camp there to see the canyon darken and mammoth arches glow in the fading light of sunset.

Wild Things

If you were an animal living among the colorful cliffs of Colorado National Monument, where would you choose to make your home? Although much of the landscape seems rocky and harsh, a hike to the Kissing Couple or a stroll along the *Alcove Nature Trail* reveals that wildlife have a surprising variety of habitats in this high desert.

Habitats range from piñon and juniper woodlands to cottonwood groves in the deep canyon bottoms. In this dry country, food such as seeds, leaves, and even other animals is easy to find, but water may be hard to come by. Thanks to thundershowers, seeps, and seasonal streams, small but precious pools of water can quench the thirst of animals such as mule deer, coyotes, and cottontails.

High Rise Habitat

Rock outcroppings not only provide cover for secretive mammals such as desert bighorn sheep and cougars, but some of the highest corners and crevices also shelter peregrine falcons. Once an endangered species, these swift hunters have made a successful comeback in Colorado.

With binoculars, patient bird-watchers can scan the cliffs for signs such as bleached droppings spilling down the stone like whitewash, which locate a scrape, or a narrow rock ledge, where the birds nest. Peregrines launch from their scrapes to stoop, or dive, on prey such as pigeons or white-throated swifts. You might even see peregrines in astounding aerobatic tumbles when they lock talons with larger birds of prey that threaten their young.

Leaping Lizards

What is green and yellow, shares the name of a canyon in the monument, and does pushups every time it's threatened? The collared lizard! Although a sighting in Lizard Canyon is not guaranteed, it is possible to encounter one of these showy reptiles in almost any canyon of the monument.

Easy to identify, collared lizards have black rings around their necks, set against a vivid backdrop of bright yellow bands, spots, and dots on their green bodies. They measure 14 inches from head to tail, and they eat insects and other small lizards. After spending winter underground, collared lizards claim a territory and defend it boldly. If disturbed, collared lizards bob up and down to warn that a chase or fight may come next. Other reptiles may capture your attention, too. Be on the lookout for side-blotched lizards, sagebrush lizards, eastern fence lizards, and whiptails, and bullsnakes, too.

Micro Scape

It's a wonder how plants can grow here. Notice in some rim areas that the soil appears dark and spongy and has a lot of lumps and bumps. This isn't soil at all, but a combination of living organisms called microbiotic crust. This collection of lichens, algae, moss, and fungi serves an important purpose in the early stages of plant development. By carpeting the earth and soaking up water, this crust slows erosion while tiny algae convert nitrogen in the air for use by more complex types of plants. Microbiotic crust is not very tough; stepping on it can destroy a decade of growth.

Back in Time Line

Did you ever like a place so much that it seemed like home the first time you saw it? John Otto felt that way the first time he saw the soaring walls of Ute and Monument Canyons. "I came here last year and found these canyons," he wrote in 1907, "and they felt like the heart of the world to me." He decided to stay where his only neighbors were golden eagles that flew eye to eye with him as he walked the canyon rims.

One Person Really Can Make A Difference

Otto was fascinated by the giant monoliths and started a one-man crusade to protect the area as a national park. He wrote letters to the federal government about the value of this sculptured landscape; he circulated a petition in Grand Junction to rally more support, and after months of correspondence, John Otto's dream came true. On May 24, 1911, U.S. President William Howard Taft established Colorado National Monument.

Otto was named the monument's first caretaker, and for only $1 a month, he was content to watch over his cherished canyon country that now belonged to the American public. Otto built trails to the grandest views so that everyone could enjoy the monument. His greatest construction was the Trail of the Serpent, a hair-raising road with 54 steep switchbacks, that snaked from the bottom of No Thoroughfare Canyon to the rim above. Today, you can stand near the Devil's Kitchen Trailhead and look up at the old highway and realize the backbreaking labor that, in 1921, allowed adventurous motorists to visit Colorado National Monument. During the 1930s, Civilian Conservation Corps workers widened some of Otto's narrow trails along the monument's rim into today's 23-mile Rim Rock Drive.

John Otto lived in the monument's colorful canyon country in the early 1900s. He promoted preservation of the area and became the monument's first caretaker. Colorado Historical Society

Monumental Decisions

National parks and national monuments protect the greatest natural and cultural treasures in the country. The main difference between the two designations is that national parks can be created only by an act of Congress; a national monument may be established on lands already owned or controlled by the U.S. government either by an act of Congress or by a presidential proclamation, without a vote by Congress.

Travel Log

• The west entrance to Colorado National Monument is reached from Interstate 70 Exit 19, at Fruita. Take Colorado 340 south to the entrance. Or, through Grand Junction, follow I-70 Business Loop to Colorado 340. Take Monument Road out of town to the east entrance. Rim Rock Drive loops around via South Broadway and South Camp Road if you want to return the way you came.

• Entrance and camping fees are charged. Saddlehorn Campground is one of the nicest places to camp in Colorado. There is also camping at nearby Bureau of Land Management recreational areas.

• The visitor center is open year-round with extended summer hours. Check here for information on backcountry excursions. Ranger-led walks and campfire talks are a highlight of any visit. Write: Colorado National Monument, Fruita, CO 81521. (970) 858-3617

• Rattlesnake Arches via Black Ridge Hunter Access Road—You need a high-clearance, four-wheel drive vehicle for this route west from the junction of Rim Rock Drive and the road to Glade Park. You should get detailed directions and current road conditions at the monument visitor center before proceeding. It's a 2-hour drive at a leisurely and safe pace along a 13-mile dirt road. Do not consider this trip in threatening weather because wet conditions make the road impassable. Camping is permitted, but no facilities are available.

• Rattlesnake Arches via *Pollock Canyon Trail*—Trailhead access is reached outside of Colorado National Monument, 1.5 miles south of Interstate 70 Exit 19, at Fruita. Turn west off Colorado 340 into Kingview Estates and continue through the development to a dirt road. The trailhead is in 4.0 miles. This 14-mile round trip is a strenuous up-and-down canyon country backpack. No drinking water or facilities exist and everything must be carried in for this overnight adventure. Before attempting this trip, contact the Bureau of Land Management, 2815 H Road, Grand Junction, CO 81506 for more information; (970) 244-3000.

3

Creede, Colorado

Discovery Zone

For more than one hundred years, blankets of snow have quieted the raucous mining boom town of Creede. But Colorado's silver mining legend, a captivating example of this country's nineteenth century history, comes to life in summer when high mountain meadows of the San Juans fill with wildflowers.

There is definitely more than a day's worth of sights to enjoy here. Remnants of mining such as old ore houses, chutes, mills, and tunnel entrances dot the hillsides. Photographic opportunities of rustic structures abound. The potential for relaxation and discovery are sky-high in Creede.

Something for Everyone

Take the17-mile Bachelor Historic Tour drive over an unpaved road suitable for passenger cars and mountain bikes; there are branches off the main road for four-wheel drive vehicles. Some of the grades, like the first grade out of town, are fairly steep and, at elevations of 9,000 feet and more, can be a bit of a workout. Whatever your mode of transportation, you must take this tour to understand what makes Creede so cool.

A tour of the Underground Mining Museum before taking the drive will give you an understanding of mining activities and help make sense of the structures and artifacts seen from the road. Along the road you will see mines, most of which are privately owned, so respect private property rights; be careful, too, because there are dangerous open shafts, unsafe buildings, and old equipment.

Once on the drive, notice the many weathered tree stumps on the hillsides, remnants of the forest harvested to build the town of Creede. You'll notice that young fir trees are reclaiming the mountain slopes from the aspen.

In addition to daytime adventures, the main street of Creede offers experiences of another sort, including a repertory theater that includes plays for kids in summer. There is an old-fashioned soda fountain, a local history museum in the old railroad depot, and several antique stores. There are some overnight accommodations in town, but be sure to make reservations ahead of time.

Bicyclists on Bachelor Historic Tour road pass the Commodore Mine ore house and chutes. Creede is a remote destination off most Colorado tourists' beaten tracks. The rewards, however, are worth the effort once you reach this historic place.

Attending the Creede Repertory Theatre is an unexpected treat that adds to the flavor of a trip to this historic town. Call for reservations so you will be sure not to miss this small theater experience. Creede Repertory Theatre

Crypto Scene

Beady eyes stare out of the darkness in the dimly lit tunnels ahead. Shine your flashlight directly toward them and they vanish! These puzzling peepers belong to "Tommyknockers," friendly little gremlins that miners know watch over them. Mysterious imps, they have been known to warn miners of cave-ins and other potential hazards.

The Life of a Miner

It can be creepy down in the tunnels, without the warmth of the sun or working with the scary prospect that a tunnel collapse may never let you see the light of day again. At the Creede Underground Mining Museum, you can find out more about this challenging lifestyle on one of the daily tours narrated by experienced miners. With more than 20 displays that show the evolution of hard rock mining techniques over the years, the mining museum will fascinate you more than you ever expected!

Such an experience is made all the richer by the fine tour conductors, some of whom were miners. Tour guide Ricky Brown has worked underground most of his life and has had nearly every bone in his body broken over the years; he also lost his teeth when he looked up just as a rock broke loose from the mine ceiling and struck him in the mouth!

Guides help you understand that a miner's day would be spent drilling blast holes in a special pattern, setting dynamite charges, blasting, and finally mucking out the ore. The work was monotonous and hard. Drills were called widow makers, and drillers were the highest paid of the miners. But the drills created a fine dust inhaled by the operators who might only work for a year or so before their lungs became so congested that they died. The $.15 an hour extra they received hardly seemed worth the prospect of certain death, but there were other miners standing in line for the job.

Underground, seams of mineral-rich ore were very easy to spot, and each day miners would drill, blast, and clean up as they followed the joints in the rocks. Ore samples were tested daily to make sure the miners were following the richest vein. At the end of their 10-hour work shifts, miners returned to the surface to rest. In the old days though the many saloons, gambling houses, and other temptations frequently left the miners with little cash to show for their hard work. They would usually try to catch a few winks before returning to the tunnels to start work all over again. Frequently, when one miner got out of his bed to go to work, another tired miner got into the same bed moments later to try to snooze in the carnival atmosphere.

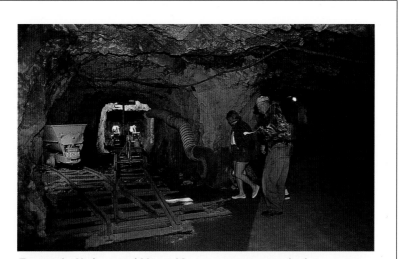

Touring the Underground Mining Museum transports you back to Colorado's silver boom. The displays are arranged to show how mining methods changed with advances in technology. Tour guides provide realism, because many once worked the tunnels.

The summer of 1890 along Creede's main street was a hectic one. People and horses crowded the street. Newspaper accounts reported that the town's population was growing by 300 people a day. Colorado Historical Society

Inspiration Point at the far end of Creede Avenue hasn't changed much over the past century—except that the crowds are gone. Some say that, late at night, the wind carries the voices of those long departed.

About 31 miles from Creede is the Wheeler Geologic Area, a rugged landscape where wind and water have sculpted haunting features in volcanic tuff. An extremely unusual site, Wheeler was a national monument for 17 years, but because it was so remote, small, and had poor access, it was returned to the U.S. Forest Service in 1950.

Bizarre Badlands

How did such a bizarre badlands end up in this high country near the Continental Divide? About 65 million years ago, ash and cinders from nearby volcanic vents were spewed into the air and deposited here. Loosely compacted ash, called tuff, has since slowly eroded into spires and pinnacles. Wheeler's weird formations have inspired names such as City of Gnomes and White Shrouded Ghosts. Just think how camping nearby during a full moon could set your imagination in motion!

The trip into the geologic area requires some preparation, especially if you are planning to camp.The road is narrow, but not steep, and winds through subalpine forest. The last 0.7 mile may be muddy and rutted. Once you reach the end of the road, a trail leads 0.6 mile to the wild formations. No motor vehicles are permitted in the geologic area. Hiking to Wheeler or going in by horseback is a 16-mile round trip from the Hanson's Mill campsite, a real endurance test for a one-day outing even though the trail is gentle and winding.

Now peaceful, Creede was once one of the wildest towns in Colorado! The town never slept, and newspaper editor Cy Warman wrote, "It's day all day in the daytime, and there is no night in Creede." An attractive place to an odd lot of people, the local newspaper stated that some of Creede's citizens "would take grubstake prize at a hog show." At one time or another, the town's population included gunman Bat Masterson and Bob Ford, the man who reputedly shot bankrobber Jesse James. A saloonkeeper, Bob Ford, died in his own saloon, shot down by Ed O'Kelly.

Ford was buried in Creede's hillside cemetery, but his body was later moved to Missouri, his home state. The now-neglected graveyard, just outside of town, with its weathered tombstones and broken down fences, shows how hard times were for its citizens: The birth and death dates on tombstones show that many of Creede's residents died young.

Creede has always been a tough little mountain town; it has survived three fires and two floods to earn its place in history. Creede was named for Nicholas C. Creede after he and another Salida prospector found a rich vein of silver ore in the area. The story goes that Nicholas yelled, "Holy Moses, I found it!" to his partner, and they called their claim the Holy Moses Mine. The town of Creede quickly grew up near the original discovery site. But it blazed only three years, between 1889 and 1893.

Happy Thought, Last Chance, Bachelor, Yankee Girl, and Kentucky Belle were a few names given to silver mines discovered by Creede prospectors. What was so special about the mining industry here? The Amethyst Mine alone yielded $2 million of ore within its first year of operation! Unfortunately, the Sherman Silver Act of 1893 caused the price of silver to drop from $1.29 an ounce to $.50 an ounce, making it unprofitable to continue to work the mines. Jubilation turned to hard scrabble for miners and families. Gradually the town's population faded away, leaving only shadows of former glory.

Ash and cinders from nearby volcanic vents were thrown into the air and carried by the wind to be deposited at the Wheeler Geologic Area. The compacted volcanic tuff has slowly eroded into sharp spires and ghostly images. These weird shapes have inspired many imaginative names, from the City of Gnomes to the White Shrouded Ghosts. Can you add any others?

There have been a couple of productive years since the turn of the century, but to make it worth mining again, the price of silver needs to be $10 to $15 per ounce in order to compete with silver mined outside the United States. Today, tons of silver ore still lie buried within the more than 2,000 miles of tunnels drilled deep into the mountains encircling Creede. It's quiet now, and the aspen and Douglas firs are reclaiming the rocky hillsides.

Travel Log

• Plan ahead for a mountain meadow picnic when you visit Creede, either from your car or mountain bike ride. Sporting goods, including mountain bikes, can be rented in town if you find you have forgotten some gear.

• Attending a performance of the Creede Repertory Theatre is a must. The plays are scheduled so that at the height of the summer season, you can see six plays in four days. There are usually four full-length productions, a one-act play, and a children's program. Call or write for the listing of programs and play dates: Creede Repertory Theatre, P.O. Box 269, Creede, CO 81130; (719) 658-2540.

• The Creede Chamber of Commerce is the best place for all the information you need to plan your visit: P.O. Box 580, Creede, CO 81130; (719) 658-2374 or (800) 327-2102.

• The Silver Thread National Scenic Byway traces the history of the silver boom by linking Creede with South Fork and Lake City. The drive is a great way to enjoy the spectacular scenery of the San Juan Mountains, especially in fall. There are historical markers along the byway and a leisurely trip along 75 miles of Colorado 149 provides a memorable one-day adventure.

4 Denver Museum of Natural History

It's snowing outside. The wind is blowing, it's cold, and the idea of being outdoors is not very appealing. Have you thought about an indoor alternative? other than the mall? Where could you go that would be interesting and fun? Is there a place that offers activities and challenges of all kinds?

It really doesn't need to be winter to seek out the Denver Museum of Natural History because the museum is fun and exciting any time of the year. Equipped with countless fascinating permanent exhibits on three floors, the museum occupies 300,000 square feet of space. That's about the area of six and one-half football fields! Dioramas, 92 of them, are among the best in the world. The museum hosts traveling exhibits from around the world, bringing strange and interesting cultures right into the city of Denver. The museum also has a theater with a movie screen 60 feet high and a sound system that pounds your senses.

Variety: The Spice of Museum Life

There is something for everyone at the Denver Museum of Natural History.

The Hall of Life on the second floor explores the wonders of human existence. When you enter the hall, you are given a magnetic card that you use at computer stations to record your strength, heart rate, blood pressure, height, weight, and age, among other statistics. There are exhibits on nutrition, the effects of stress and drugs, and tips on how to improve your health. Other displays and a film explore the beginning of life and the growth of a human baby. If the genetic code of life has been a mystery to you, check out the exhibit that helps you unravel the double helix of a strand of DNA. Then you can learn how chemical codes pass traits from one generation to the next. At the end of the Hall of Life, you are given a health profile about yourself and the results of the tests you took during your trip through the exhibit hall!

"Prehistoric Journey, a Walk Through Time" explores the origins of life and stitches together evidence scientists have found in the field. There are 14 complete dinosaur skeletons and skeletons from the age of mammals, the Miocene epoch. The discoveries and observations you may make at other cool places in Colorado, such as the dinosaur tracks at Picket Wire Canyonlands, will come into sharp focus in the Cretaceous Creekbed exhibit. Don't be distracted

The Denver Museum of Natural History is rich with opportunities for discovery. Its exhibits invite you to explore far-off places or your own backyard.

by the big "pig" nearby, though. Its roar is worse than its bite. The museum staff spent seven years planning and constructing Prehistoric Journey at a cost of $7 million.

Paleontologists are scientists who dig into the past. When you stand at the window of the Earth Sciences Laboratory at the end of Prehistoric Journey, you can watch detective work in progress. In this fossil lab, highly trained volunteers and professionals work side by side, painstakingly cleaning dirt and rock from around fossils brought back from the field. The rock material, or matrix, that encases a fossil must be removed carefully so that critical evidence such as skin impressions, small bones, and plant remains are not destroyed. Magnifying lenses and closed-circuit television monitors allow you to observe the technicians at work as they reveal clues about the past before your eyes. Fossil preparation is slow and exacting work. If you are good with details, being a fossil preparator may just be in your future!

The Colorado Hall offers an opportunity to sample an excellent cross section of the state. It features tons of interactive exhibits that help to sharpen your knowledge of the state's natural history.

Also, check out the lecture series and special museum tours to all sorts of interesting places, such as the airline pilot training facility at the old Stapleton Airport. This special field trip lets you see state-of-the-art flight simulators that help pilots learn different emergency procedures and become better versed in the aircraft they fly.

One of the museum's more unusual offerings is the opportunity for a family camp-in. This popular program is offered each fall, and the lucky few families who sign up in time receive special behind-the-scenes tours of the museum. Special overnights can also be arranged for school groups.

Perhaps the best features of the Denver Museum of Natural History are the dioramas. These meticulously fabricated re-creations of habitats from four continents whisk you away to far-off places in a moment. You can stand on the wind-swept plains of Africa at a watering hole or view a colony of elephant seals on a barren island off New Zealand. Inquire at the museum about special tours of the habitat laboratories where the realism of the world is created with common household materials!

The museum is a very full, almost exhausting, day of exploration. If you need to take a break and to regain your energy, stop at the T-Rex Delicatessen. Having lunch or a snack under the three-story-high ceiling and watching the hustle and bustle of museum visitors is fun in itself. But it's the dino delights you will remember most. When is the last time you tried a B.L.T-Rex sandwich or munched on a Veggiesaurus?

Paleo Scene

Prehistoric Journey is the newest and best series of dioramas at the museum. Enjoy the exhibit by first watching a short time-travel film that takes you back to the origins of life on our planet. Time travel begins in the sea and moves to the shore, following the footsteps of the earliest land dwelling animals. From that point, the world seems to explode with a series of great experiments in life forms, both plant and animal, and various methods of survival.

Dinosaurs lurk just after the "Forests and Flight" exhibit. Examining the skeletons and artists' re-creations of skin and colors, your imagination can transports you back more than 70 million years. You cannot help but wonder what it would have been like to see these magnificent creatures moving through primeval forests or what sounds they made searching for prey.

The fossils in this hall have been collected from many places in the West. Even though the fossil record may be sketchy in one location, the entire collection gives us a glimpse into the past. The jump from fossil specimens to the real world outside is not very great. Use the information you gather here to help you make better observations and discoveries as you explore Colorado. You will find that many significant discoveries of dinosaurs have been made here. In fact, a group of high school students discovered a stegosaur skeleton while on a field trip, and fourth grade students from Thornton successfully initiated the process to have the stegosaur designated the official state fossil.

Numerous publications can guide you to areas known to have dinosaur remains. It is always a good idea to know the regulations that pertain to the public land you are exploring. Remember, it is critical to our understanding of these creatures that, if you find a fossil or make a discovery, you report your

What a reception! The 20-foot-tall Tyrannosaurus rex *steps through 80 million years to welcome visitors to the halls of prehistoric life and many other adventures at the Denver Museum of Natural History.*

A ferocious-looking entelodont hides in the Nebraska woodland exhibit along the Prehistoric Journey Trail. It sounds more real than it is!

find to a museum or university. This way, professionals can examine the site to determine how important it might be to learning more about dinosaurs. Document your find by photographing, sketching, and recording the location so you can locate it again. Vertebrate fossils are protected on federal land, and it is illegal to dig or collect such remnants of ancient life that you may find in national forests and recreation areas, at national parks or monuments, or lands managed by other federal agencies.

Crypto Scene

Are the animals real? That is the most frequently asked question by people standing in front of museum dioramas. Most of the animals are real and were collected years before people became more sensitive about conserving wildlife. However, naturalists needed to study animals closely in order to understand them as we do today. Some collecting continues, but not as much as in the early days of the museum. Animal lovers are happy to know that most of the new displays contain models of real animals.

How does the museum staff make the scenes so real and where is such work done? What tricks do they use to fool the eye when you look at dioramas?

Get the Behind-the-Scenes Scoop

The Habitats Laboratory staff's work is exciting and challenging. In the museum's basement is a space for the creative people who develop and

An exhibit specialist examines a re-creation of elephant dung for placement in a diorama.

From behind the scenes the elephant seals of Campbell Island diorama looks a bit unfinished.

maintain the diorama exhibits. Depending on what project is underway, the work space can expand to accommodate the pieces of a display as complex as Prehistoric Journey, or shrink to just enough room to re-create a portion of Colorado prairie.

There are so many elements included in each display that a team of specialists is required to create a diorama. Planning begins with the education department of the museum; designers sketch out the ideas for the exhibit, and curators identify specimens that could be included. Not so long ago, the museum would make expeditions to obtain specimens if they did not have the animals they needed. Such an expedition was made to Campbell Island in the South Pacific in 1957 to obtain elephant seals and to collect information to re-create a scene from the island habitat accurately.

Murals painted on the back walls of dioramas are critical to successful re-creations and the Habitats Lab creates rocks and plants to place in the foreground. Today, rocks are mostly fiberglass, but smaller grasses and bushes are real. After the plants are dried, they are spray painted to keep them looking fresh. Larger plants and trees are often made of plaster or plastic and painted to look lifelike.

Taxidermists begin to prepare animals by making sure the specimens are in a natural pose. To achieve this, they start with an armature, or frame in the shape of the animal being prepared. The hide is draped over the frame and sewn together, with the seam cleverly hidden from view.

Museum specialists rely on tricks to deceive you. In the elephant seals of Campbell Island exhibit, the seal in the rear, on the far right side of the diorama, is fiberglass. Another example of deception is that only the fronts of large trees may be painted, while the backs are hollow. All the while, museum visitors feel they are gazing at a solid section of rain forest!

In a third floor exhibit, featuring a cheetah chasing two impalas, look carefully at the dust raised by the cheetah as it tries to catch its prey. Do you have any idea how this illusion was created? The "dust" is actually painted plastic. From the visitor's perspective, the dust looks real! However, when viewed from the side, it looks like ordinary plastic wrap!

Just down the hall, in the Savuti Water Hole exhibit, look carefully at the shadows under the zebras. Are they real shadows? Tricked again. The exhibits staff pigmented the sand below the animal to duplicate a natural shadow—day or night! When museum personnel enter the diorama, they strap on special shoe covers with hoofprints on the soles so they can walk on the dirt floors without leaving any human footprints!

The Habitats Lab work is often very tedious. For example, there are 2 million wax leaves on the trees and small bushes in the Moose and Caribou diorama—each one created by hand! This diorama took five years to complete and required the work of hundreds of volunteers. The Alaska exhibit has one of the best illusions. It makes you feel as though you are standing on a hill overlooking a vast plain, but the exhibit is only 12 feet deep.

Sometimes exhibit preparators become playful. In one diorama, an artist painted himself as a small leprechaun waving goodbye. It was his last exhibit background to paint, and this was his farewell to the visitors. Can you find the artist's special signature on your visit to the museum?

Micro Scape

Museum archaeologists were excavating a site near Folsom, New Mexico, in 1926 when they uncovered an unusually shaped stone projectile point, or arrowhead, in association with bison bones. This stone point was an important discovery for two reasons. Once authenticated, the point confirmed the presence of human activity in North America 8,000 years earlier than had been known before. Distinctively shaped, the projectile was given the name Folsom point. Similar discoveries later helped to date cultural periods of use throughout the Southwest.

Museums frequently trade specimens and archaeological items that are considered very valuable by other museums. The Folsom point discovery, as well as an archaeological excavation at Dent, Colorado, provided important leverage for the museum: These findings allowed the Denver museum to trade for a *Diplodocus* and an *Antatosaurus*.

The first wing of the Denver Museum of Natural History, completed in 1903, was opened to the public in 1908. The museum was quite a distance from downtown Denver then. Colorado Boulevard had not yet been paved and ranchers drove their cows down the middle of the street to the livestock market!

The museum was the dream of Edwin Carter, a naturalist, who had a collection of more than 3,000 animals from all over Colorado. Carter died in 1900, before the museum opened its doors to the public, but through the efforts of others, his dream of a natural history museum became a reality and an exciting place for you to visit.

Throughout its 90-year history, the museum has relied on and benefited from the generosity of many people. This tradition continues today and has grown even stronger. The original 22 museum supporters have multiplied more than 1,000 times and includes people from all walks of life. The volunteer program encourages people of all ages (the minimum age for volunteers is 13) to contribute to the museum's growth. If you are interested in working with special traveling exhibits or with any of the many departments of the museum, the staff could really use your help, and you might find that work can be fun!

An African water hole is the museum setting for a school camp-in.

Travel Log

•   The Denver Museum of Natural History is in City Park, at 2001 Colorado Boulevard, adjacent to the Denver Zoo. The park is a great place to have a picnic, though the museum has a deli and cafeteria. There is an admission to the museum and entry into the IMAX theater is separate. Gates Planetarium offers programs all year with laser light shows set to music and seasonal star programs. The book and gift shop has a great selection of items associated with the museum's educational themes.

•   The museum staff lead many interesting trips and offer special behind-the-scenes tours at the museum and to interesting locations around the state. The lecture series covers a broad range of topics and armchair adventures to exotic locations.

•   Consider purchasing a membership if you plan to visit often. With the pass, the museum is free and there are substantial discounts for the IMAX theater, special tours, lectures, and the gift store. Watch for traveling exhibits hosted by the museum; some exhibitions often visit only a few U.S. cities.

5 Dinosaur National Monument

Discovery Zone

It's summer, and it's hot, very hot in the northwest corner of Colorado. Split Mountain juts above the horizon like the bow of a ship sinking into the Green River below. It's quiet, very quiet. The sun bakes the sandstone and shale scenery. Dust kicks up along a ridge, as it has for thousands of years, swirling in circles around each crack in the rock, each fissure in time.

Dinosaur National Monument seems a forbidding place for a treasure hunt. But the rocks around the Dinosaur Quarry building are like an X on a pirate's map. Riches found here were not doubloons and jewels, though. The Dinosaur Quarry, an angular glass and steel building, shelters remains of colossal animals that lived 150 million years ago, when the land was not quite so dry and desert-like. Now more valuable to science than any precious stones, the fossils of giant dinosaurs lie exposed on a tilted slab of rock.

An Unbelievable Gallery of Bones

Boarding a shuttle to the monument's Dinosaur Quarry, visitors ascend the sandstone bluffs that lured paleontologists to the Colorado-Utah border almost one hundred years ago. Although nearly a century has passed and hundreds of fossils have been unearthed, excitement and anticipation still capture the imagination as visitors embark on their own discovery of Dinosaur.

Inside the building that now covers the quarry, an imposing gray rock wall draws visitors like a magnet. Here you can touch a fossil leg bone and begin to understand how this place captivated those first scientists. What did they think when they first saw a bone like this? In their excitement, could they say or do anything at all?

The Dinosaur Quarry covers the excavated remains of dinosaurs. The slanted rock wall is like a big grocery store of bones. Visitors browse for their favorite bit of stegosaur or apatosaur. Most of the immense slab is beyond reach, but the fossils are so big and abundant that they still amaze visitors.

Over the years, more than 20 complete dinosaur skeletons were excavated from the quarry. Specimens of 12 species of Jurassic plant-eaters and meat-eaters were extracted and shipped to institutions such as the Carnegie Museum in Pittsburgh, Pennsylvania, and the Smithsonian in Washington, D.C. Although specimens are no longer removed from the quarry wall, you can see

A shuttle drops visitors at the Dinosaur Quarry.

paleontologists at work in the laboratory using sophisticated tools to reveal details of more recent finds. Once a specimen is cleaned and bared as much as possible, it is soaked with a protective varnish.

Painstaking work has revealed bony plates of a stegosaur, scattered after millions of years, along with the giant, snaking spine of an apatosaur (also known as a brontosaur), and the sharp claws of a carnivorous allosaur. The entire slab contains an astounding mishmash of arms, legs, tails, and toes, which together, form a most awesome display of fossilized dinosaur bones.

Dinosaur's Diversity
Surprisingly, Dinosaur National Monument has much more to offer than fantastic fossils. You should definitely plan to stay longer than one day. There are 330 square miles of dramatically carved canyon country waiting to be explored.
• Hit the Trail—Since much of Dinosaur is steep and remote, the National Park Service has established marked trails in some of the best spots. Next to rushing water, the 8-mile round trip *Jones Hole Trail* takes serious hikers off to enjoy the solitude of the powerful Green River, while shorter trails off Harpers Corner Road and Cub Creek Road offer easier access to the natural and geologic history of the monument.
• Roads by Bike or Car—Save a day for every road you want to travel in the monument because each one offers something different! The Tilted Rocks tour on Cub Creek Road is a good way to spend a day. This self-guided, 22-mile round-trip will give you close-up views of the Green River and Split Mountain, and large Fremont Indian petroglyphs. Farther east, Harpers Corner Road

Harpers Corner Scenic Drive offers great views of the heart of Dinosaur.

presents outstanding views, while dirt roads to Echo Park and Yampa Bench take drivers off the beaten path.

• Dinosaur by Boat—The Yampa and the Green Rivers meet deep in the heart of the national monument. It takes three to five days to enjoy the canyon bends by kayak, raft, or dory with experienced guides. Nothing compares to the serenity of a starlit sky over the wild, free-flowing Yampa River or the thrill of the crashing rapids on the Green's Canyon of Lodore.

• Spend the Night—Now that you know there is so much to see and do at Dinosaur, you should take your camping gear along! Not far from the Dinosaur Quarry, Green River Campground nestles in a grove of cottonwoods next to the river. Farther east, a great view of Steamboat Rock rewards drivers who make the 13-mile journey down Harpers Corner Road to Echo Park Campground, while Deerlodge Park is a popular stopover for those venturing onto the Yampa River.

Paleo Scene

Why are hundreds of dinosaur fossils so perfectly preserved here and what do rivers have to do with them?

About 150 million years ago, long before the Uinta Mountains developed, the jagged landscape we now know as Dinosaur National Monument was a broad, flat floodplain. Slow-moving rivers and streams channeled through sandy soils where plants such as ferns, cycads, or palmlike plants, and conifers grew in semi-arid Jurassic conditions. Perfect sauropod, or plant-eating dinosaur, habitat, this low-lying plain was home for *Apatosaurus, Camarasaurus, Diplodocus,* and other such dinosaurs, including *Stegosaurus.*

Of course, where vegetarians wandered, sharp-toothed carnivores followed —meat-eating theropods that ran on two legs, such as *Allosaurus* and *Ceratosaurus.* Mixed into this menagerie were crocodiles, freshwater clams, turtles, and at least one kind of frog.

Most dinosaurs died without leaving a trace, but in one bend of the ancient river, conditions for preservation prevailed. Floodwaters carried dinosaur remains downstream, where they lodged in sand at the bend and were buried rapidly. Some carcasses were buried quickly, some more slowly, when rising waters covered the bodies with sand and mud, allowing the process of fossilization to begin. Unfortunately, strong currents tangled, bent, or broke some of the bodies. Over the years, layers of sand thousands of feet deep were deposited over the Morrison Formation—the final resting place of the dead dinosaurs. Water then dissolved silica that filtered into the dinosaur skeletons cell by cell, mineralizing the bones while the surrounding sand turned to rock.

This dinosaur bone bed would have remained hidden forever if the Rocky Mountains had not formed to the east about 65 million years ago. As the Continental Divide rose higher and higher, dinosaur country warped and tilted, not from the uplift of the Rockies but by being squeezed and shifted along fault lines. The bones stayed entombed until millions of years of erosion finally revealed them in the sandstone ridge now sheltered by the Dinosaur Quarry.

Inside the Dinosaur Quarry, visitors can touch the smooth surface of a huge dinosaur leg-bone fossil. Hundreds more fossils lie exposed in the tilted slab of rock that makes up one side of the building. Impressive pieces of deceased stegosaurs and apatosaurs seem to litter the gray chunk of rock that once was the bottom of a bend in a prehistoric river.

Crypto Scene

"Fire in the hole!"
Boom!
Ash-gray rock explodes into the cool winter air. When the dust settles and the chief blaster shouts "All Clear!" crew members then walk back to inspect the excavation site. Excitement like this has not occurred here since the turn of the century, when paleontologist Earl Douglass made the first discovery of dinosaur fossils in the region.

Dinosaur's New Dinosaur

In a narrow canyon, not far from the historic discovery site, park paleontologist Dan Chure noticed something unusual about the sandstone wall positioned at least 20 feet above the floor of the wash. What prize could nature have uncovered now? The answer? Dinosaur toes! And part of a tail, too!

That one day in 1990 has meant seven years of patient work to identify a new species of dinosaur. At first, no one knew how much more of the dinosaur might be found in the cliff. Three years of careful excavation finally revealed that this was a special specimen. Originally thought to be a meat-eating *Allosaurus*, paleontologists were excited to find that the fossil was nearly complete and articulated, with the bones naturally positioned, almost as if they were still connected by living tissue! Many questions arose about the new find that could only be answered by closer scientific examination.

Three hundred tons of rock had to be blasted and excavated to isolate the 8-foot-tall, 20-foot-long fossil in a 6,700-pound block of rock. Then it needed to be transported to the paleontology laboratory in the Dinosaur Quarry. The dinosaur was protected in a wrap of burlap and plaster and helicoptered 0.5 mile to the Quarry building.

Paleontologists then began the painstaking work of picking pounds of sandstone away from the delicate fossil. Their research suggested this was not your average *Allosaurus!* Presumably a new dinosaur species, the fossil at least deserved a nickname: It became known as NAA, for Not-an-*Allosaurus*.

Not-an-*Allosaurus* could not tell its whole story because it had lost its head somewhere along the way. To locate NAA's skull would be like finding the missing page of a mystery novel giving the critical clue; it would support conclusions about what kind of dinosaur it might be. Driven to solve this puzzle, paleontologists enlisted radiologist Ray Jones, an x-ray expert from the University of Utah. Jones had developed a special machine to detect gamma particles (tiny magnetic structures linked to carbon atoms) that are sometimes emitted from fossilized bone. Jones measured the gamma emissions at NAA's excavation site to see if more bones might be found. In July 1996, the determined scientist found a high gamma reading in rock near where the rest of the skeleton had been found. The missing treasure had been discovered! Weeks of excavation and another helicopter airlift brought the skull back to the lab for study.

The skull, two feet long, with nasty spikes for teeth, resembles an

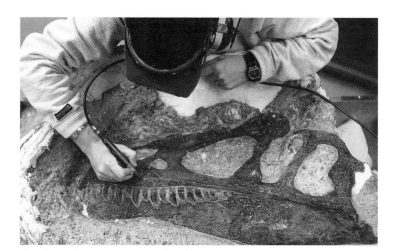

*A paleontologist uses a special tool to remove rock from the fossilized skull of Not-an-*Allosaurus. *The two-foot long skull matches the headless skeleton of one of the monument's most recent dinosaur discoveries.*
National Park Service

Allosaurus skull, but its bone structure is quite different. Paleontologists, with microscopes, used miniature jackhammers to remove rock from around the fossil. Tedious work revealed that the left side of the large skull was intact, but only a portion of the right side remained. Because previous work proved NAA's body was missing a right arm, scientists think that the dinosaur came to rest on its left side in the riverbed and currents swept away its missing parts.

Plans for Not-an-*Allosaurus* include further preparation, then assemblage of the skeleton with the skull. Park visitors can observe paleontologists at work in the Dinosaur Quarry laboratory, where the nearly complete NAA will some-day be displayed.

Wild Things

The canyons of the Green and Yampa Rivers support intersting wild things, from rare Ute ladies tresses orchids to native Colorado squawfish and Mexican spotted owls.

Rain is generally scarce in this region, yet when it falls, it comes down hard, scouring gullies and canyons where some populations of rare plants and animals live. Less naturally, dam releases upstream on the Green River send frigid water along that favor nonnative trout, making survival tough for native chubs, suckers, and squawfish.

The Yampa, in contrast to the Green, is a free-flowing river, and offers the opportunity to study a canyon in its natural state. Spring floods are the most important element lost on dammed rivers. Such seasonal rises in water are necessary to deposit soil and replenish the rich riparian, or streamside, habitat for wildlife. Although some animals such as deer mice and kangaroo rats can be washed away during floods, most animals benefit. Visit the Yampa and Green; see if you notice significant differences between the controlled Green River and the free-flowing Yampa.

Micro Scape

Not all dinosaurs were 80-ton beasts lumbering in Jurassic jungles. Big bones had the best chance for preservation, so few collections have specimens of smaller dinosaurs. Rocks at Dinosaur National Monument contain significant clues about some smaller creatures, specimens so tiny that they are almost invisible to the naked eye!

Some of these small fossils include the razor-sharp teeth of meat-eating dinosaurs that stood just 19 inches tall. Only one-fifth of an inch long, such specimens require study with the help of scanning electron microscopes. These tools can be used to photograph fossils so minute that they fit on the head of a

*Dinosaur displays in the Quarry build-
ing capture the visitor's attention.*

*Whispering Cave is an intriguing stop
along the dirt road to Echo Park.*

pin! Results show unusual features on the teeth that indicate possible new species. Teeth with knifelike edges probably enabled these dinosaurs to eat small mammals or lizards that shared their prehistoric floodplain habitat.

Back in Time Line

Over the years Earl Douglass studied plants in Mexico, discovered mammal fossils in Montana, developed dendrochronology, the technique of tree-ring dating, and worked for the Carnegie Museum in Pittsburgh, Pennsylvania. But, none of his interesting experiences compared to the thrilling discovery he made on a ragged ridgetop in 1909.

Working in Utah as a paleontologist for the Carnegie Museum, Douglass was sent to an area of exposed rocks in search of specimens for the museum's collection. An expert fossil-finder, Douglass knew that this spiny hogback of Morrison Formation rocks could contain dinosaur bones. He also understood that the hunt might not pay off at all.

Beginning his pursuit in 1908, Douglass looked for signs of oddly shaped stone embedded in solid rock or protruding from softer shales. On August 17, 1909, the discovery of a lifetime made this paleontologist's dream come true. As if it had whipped around the rocks just yesterday, the tail of a *Brontosaurus* lay in the top of the Morrison ledge. Douglass described the eight tail bones as "a beautiful sight"—a treasure that led him and his workers to dig out thousands of fossil dinosaur bones from the ridge for the next 15 years.

Public interest in this one-of-a-kind site resulted in the establishment of Dinosaur National Monument in 1915. After several years of unearthing complete and partial fossil skeletons, Douglass left much of the remaining sandstone face intact for generations of dinosaur enthusiasts to enjoy.

Travel Log

• It takes most of a day to travel to Dinosaur National Monument from Denver. Beyond Craig, U.S. 40 passes through high desert. Dinosaur is the closest town to monument headquarters. A 25-mile drive takes visitors to Jensen, then north seven miles on Colorado 149 to the Dinosaur Quarry. Monument headquarters is open daily in summer and only weekdays in winter. The Dinosaur Quarry is open year-round, except January 1, Thanksgiving, and December 25. Entrance fees are charged.

• There are six fee-area campgrounds; one is reserved for groups. Gasoline is available in Dinosaur, Colorado, and Jensen, Utah. Vernal, Utah and Craig, Colorado have additional services, including lodging.

• Echo Park and Yampa Bench Roads are suitable for most passenger cars during dry conditions, but are impassable when wet.

• The Dinosaur Quarry is the only place to view fossils in the monument. Collecting fossils or any other artifacts is prohibited.

6
The Flat Tops

Discovery Zone

There is nothing like this place east of the Continental Divide! The Flat Tops offer adventure, unusual mountain scenery, and impressive aspen forests. When you think you have seen all of Colorado, you finally head to the Flat Tops. Then you wonder why you didn't visit sooner.

A trip to the Flat Tops, mountains on national forest lands north of Interstate 70 between Dotsero and New Castle, is a journey into the wilderness where cascades flow down from dark rock amphitheaters and course through lush green mountain meadows and woodlands. Fish leap from lakes sparkling in the summer sun. From the spectacular canyon of Deep Creek in the south to the serenity of Trappers Lake in the north, the Flat Tops are an unforgettable destination for anyone with a passion for nature.

County and graveled forest service roads of the Flat Tops Trail Scenic Byway, between the tiny town of Yampa, on the east, and Meeker, on the west, take you through rolling foothills past one of the first homesteads in the Yampa Valley. Along this incredibly scenic route, the striking 10,000-foot Flat Tops mark the way across 9,763-foot Dunckley Pass to the valley of the North Fork of the White River. Miles and miles of white-barked aspen line this stretch of road to Trappers Lake, where camping, fishing, hiking, and horseback riding attract outdoor enthusiasts.

Land of the Lakes

A network of trails surrounds 313-acre Trappers Lake in the Flat Tops. You can practically drive to the lake, but it is a wilderness area—no motors are allowed. Anglers at Scotts Bay parking area carry every kind of motorless boat imaginable to the lake, from inflatable sea kayaks to personal belly boats. The reward is unbelievable peace and quiet and the chance to catch some of the only native Colorado River cutthroat trout in the United States.

Floating, fishing, and photography all have one thing in common at Trappers Lake: the awesome backdrop of the Chinese Wall and the Amphitheater. All eyes are drawn to the heights of these massive rock walls. What is it like up there on the Flat Tops?

• To Big Fish Lake—Himes Peak Campground, just off Forest Road 205 to Trappers Lake, offers one of the best starting points for first-time hikers into

From Dunckley Pass, the Flat Tops draw visitors into the heart of unspoiled wilderness. Acres of thick aspen forests flank the high plateau that is made up of dark volcanic rock carved by glaciers.

the Flat Tops Wilderness. A bridge over the North Fork of the White River leads hikers, backpackers, and horseback riders along a 3-mile route through meadows and subalpine forests to Big Fish Lake, nestled at the base of a towering rock amphitheater. An overnight stay near this beautiful bowl is one of the best in the Rockies.

• To Twin Lakes—Beyond Big Fish Lake, the trail gets tough. On a hot day, hikers gulp down plenty of water while they hike past downed timber around Florence Lake, a favorite hangout for mosquitoes. A couple of hard miles more and you're at a small pass that opens up to a vast, flat, lake-dotted, grassy expanse that looks like the world's biggest and highest golf course! The only features higher are Big Marvine and Trappers Peak, around 12,000 feet in elevation. From here, it's practically a stroll to Twin Lakes or any of the other hundreds of shimmering gems of the Flat Tops Wilderness.

• To Wall Lake—The trail to Wall Lake takes off from a parking area near the campgrounds at Trappers Lake. This is about the quickest way to the top and follows a stream through a lovely forested valley to a terrace on the rock wall beyond. A final push up a steep grade ends with a classic Flat Tops vista of meadows and lakes. In less than 4 miles, Wall Lake is a good place for a base camp to make easier walks along the plateau. A great day on the Flat Tops may include a swim in one of the smaller lakes—a shallow one that's warmed up in the summer sun—along the trail.

Paleo Scene

It took millions of years for volcanoes, earthquakes, and glaciers to create today's Flat Tops. Formations with names such as the Chinese Wall and the Devil's Causeway testify to the powerful geologic events that shaped the area.

During the Tertiary Period, 3 to 65 million years ago, the earth rumbled and split, spewing molten lava across what is now the White River Plateau. Uplifts followed, heaving the solid caprock and its underlying sediments above the surrounding landscape. Pleistocene, or Ice Age, glaciers carved U-shaped valleys into the high, flat, lava plateau, leaving behind spectacular amphitheaters and crystalline lakes. An irregular border of dark lava remains as a distinct outline of the present Flat Top Mountains.

Crypto Scene

A mystery awaits backcountry travelers on the plateau. There are miles and miles of silvery forest. Why? In the 1940s, voracious spruce bark beetles attacked 68,000 acres of Englemann spruce woodlands. Trees killed by the beetles bleached and weathered in the Colorado sun. Almost 60 years later, the ghost forest remains; be wary when moving through these areas, where downed logs may block trails and trees threaten to crash. Life is reemerging in this phantom forest. Sapling spruce and alpine fir grow alongside skeletons of the silvery snags.

Wild Things

Wildlife viewing in the Flat Tops is simple. Keep your eyes open and binoculars handy. You won't be disappointed. Sometimes weasels scurry across the byway. Mule deer pass through sunny groves of aspens. Marmots waddle to the tops of boulders to watch you. But two animals are the highlight here: elk and fish.

The Flat Tops provide habitat for the largest elk herd in Colorado. Numbering into the thousands, these large members of the deer family thrive on rich meadow grasses and seek shelter in dense forests. However, summer visitors to the Flat Tops may never see any elk because the animals go to the plateau to escape insects and the warmer temperatures of the valleys. In fall, hunting is allowed in some parts of the Flat Tops, so the elk generally shy away from humans.

Because much of the rugged Flat Tops are a protected wilderness area, the lakes and streams are relatively free of the effects of most human activities. The headwaters of the White and Yampa Rivers offer ideal aquatic habitat for insects and other organisms that provide food for native cutthroat trout. When the snow melts and the waters warm up, greedy cutthroats dart along the shallows of Trappers Lake to gulp bugs by the dozens.

Yellow-bellied marmots live in meadows around Trappers Lake where lush vegetation provides plenty of nutrition. Sleek, thick fur and stores of fat help marmots survive winter hibernation.

Flowing from Trappers Outlet, the North Fork of the White River provides choice family fishing. Horseback riding is also a favorite activity for visitors in the Flat Tops.

Named Colorado's state fish in 1994, cutthroat trout have made a great recovery after decades of overfishing, competition from introduced, or non-native, trout, and loss of habitat. Rare and beautiful, Colorado River cutthroat are considered a species of special concern, but they are making a successful comeback on the Western Slope. In fact, the Flat Tops Wilderness is one of the few natural hatcheries for native Colorado River cutthroat trout left. By practicing good catch-and-release fishing techniques, novice and experienced anglers alike contribute to the cutthroat trout's promising future.

Micro Scape

In the 1800s, tremendous fires burned the region's spruce-fir forests, opening up thousands of acres to colonization by aspen. Today the aspen groves of the Flat Tops grow lush beyond compare.

Like perfectly straight, bright white guideposts, aspen come in various sizes. Depending on their age or on moisture conditions, aspen may grow close together or widely spaced, as well as tall or stunted and short. Aspen may grow as off-shoots from lateral roots from one tree, producing groups of pencil-thin suckers or from tiny seeds with long, silky hairs. Suckers are the first aspens to regenerate a forest after a fire, avalanche, logging, or some other disturbance.

All aspen that grow from one set of roots are clones, or a group of genetically identical individuals. As a result, trees from the same roots have similar attributes. For example, cloned aspens will sprout leaves at the same time in the spring. In the fall, some cloned aspens may display salmon-tinted leaves while the group next to it shimmers a bright gold. From a distance, these family units of aspen create a patchwork quilt of color, making autumn a fantastic time to travel the Flat Tops.

The aspen understory is interesting as well. Where soils are rich and moisture is high, plant growth under the aspens seems almost tropical. On some north-facing slopes in the Vaughn Lake area, dark green bracken ferns cover the ground like a jungle. Other Flat Top aspens may shelter wild roses and hundreds of sky-blue Colorado columbines or profusions of stout cow parsnip. All of these plants provide plentiful food for many mammals ranging from rodents to mule deer and elk.

Signs of Life

Aspen trunks show scars made by wildlife. Black bears sometimes claw the trunks when they climb in search of tender foliage or for bird nests. Elk and deer damage aspen trunks, too, when they gnaw the bark when food is scarce. Large circular or oval marks on lower aspen trunks are a sure sign that elk have been browsing on them.

Deep notches or pointed stubs of trunks are the work of beaver that use aspen to dam streams and build lodges. Beaver also make a meal of aspen; a beaver may eat nearly 1,500 pounds of aspen per year—about 200 trees! Less

Aspen forests in the Flat Tops furnish food and habitat for a great variety of plants and animals. Some of the best displays of Colorado columbines can be seen here during summer.

damaging to aspen are birds such as red-naped sapsuckers, flickers, and hairy woodpeckers that hollow out openings to find sap or insects. Swallows, wrens, and northern pygmy owls may follow to nest in the cavities.

So much evidence of wildlife makes aspen bark look like a puzzle. However, much of what happens to the bark is the result of injuries to branches, bacterial infections, or dark, natural openings that allow air exchange through the trunk. Even though aspen trunks are not green, they carry on some photosynthesis, just as leaves do, producing sugar for tree growth from sunlight, minerals, and water. This extra boost may help aspen recover from the many effects of wildlife and weather.

What Makes Them Quake?

As if all of these special features are not enough to make aspens unique, there is one other characteristic that singles out these trees: They seem to quake. What causes the heart-shaped leaves of these graceful trees to tremble in the slightest of breezes? The flattened stem of an aspen leaf is perpendicular, or sideways, to the leaf plane, or surface. When the leaf catches an air current, it flutters rather than bends, as it would if supported by a parallel stem, which is why they are sometimes called quaking aspen.

Ute Indians shared the Flat Tops with occasional trappers and explorers until 1878 when Nathan Meeker, a government Indian agent, was sent to the White River Valley. Meeker intended to civilize the nomadic Utes by making them farm. Friction between Meeker and the Indians resulted in the death of Meeker and 10 government employees. The Utes who lived on the White River were eventually removed from their traditional hunting and fishing grounds in the Flat Tops and placed on a reservation in Utah.

Settlers started to move in and profit from the natural resources, and by 1891, President William Henry Harrison had established the 1.2-million-acre White River Plateau Timberland Reserve, the first of its kind in Colorado, and only the second in the nation. Reorganized into a national forest in 1905, the Flat Tops attracted enough tourists to prompt the federal government to plan recreational development at Trappers Lake.

If landscape architect Arthur H. Carhart had not appreciated the beauty of Trappers Lake, there would be countless cabins and roads encircling the lake today. In 1919, the Forest Service hired Carhart to advise on development plans, but he was so impressed by the unspoiled nature of Trappers Lake that he recommended it be left in its original state. If there were to be development, it should only occur at least a half-mile from its shore. The idea to preserve such a place in its wild condition had never been heard of before!

Anglers haul boats to Trappers Lake. Trappers Peak looms like a sentinel above the wilderness trail to the lake.

Government policy eventually changed to establish wilderness preserves and other types of protected areas. The Flat Tops Primitive Area was designated in 1929 but did not include Trappers Lake. By 1975, the lake was added and the Flat Tops was reclassified as wilderness. Known now as Cradle of the Wilderness for its inspiration to Arthur H. Carhart, a father of the wilderness movement, Trappers Lake is still wild and free for everyone to enjoy.

Travel Log

• The Flat Tops Trail Scenic and Historic Byway starting from Meeker in the west, or Yampa to the east, leads into the heart of the Flat Tops. Depending on snow, the gravel road is open from June through October. The drive takes about 2.5 hours; Buford, about halfway, has gas and other services.

There are 16 national forest fee-area campgrounds along the byway as well as others in the Deep Creek area of the White River Plateau off Coffee Pot Road northwest of Dotsero. More than 300 miles of trails traverse the Flat Tops, offering hikers, packers, and horseback riders many opportunities. Mountain bikers and ATVs are allowed only on designated nonwilderness trails. Closed to automobiles in winter, the Flat Tops Trail Scenic and Historic Byway receives between 2 to 10 feet of snow, attracting cross-country skiers and snowmobilers.

• For information contact: Blanco Ranger District, White River National Forest, 317 East Market, Meeker, CO 81641; or Yampa District, Medicine Bow–Routt National Forest, P.O. Box 7, Yampa, CO 80483.

• A self-issued permit is required at wilderness trailhead registers. Information on Leave No Trace backcountry practices, water purification, pets, and special wilderness regulations is available from all U.S. Forest Service ranger stations.

• Valid Colorado state fishing or hunting licenses are required.

7
Florissant Fossil Beds

Discovery Zone

What kind of natural disaster could snap a 13-foot-thick tree like a toothpick? What incredible events could trap thousands of plants and insects beneath layer after layer of silt, preserving them forever in solid stone?

Suffocating volcanic eruptions could, especially if they occurred again and again over 700,000 years. Could such a catastrophe happen in Colorado? Yes, and it did—about 35 million years ago. Unbelievable as it may seem, the peaceful mountains just 35 miles west of Colorado Springs once bubbled with lava and darkened the sky with clouds of hot ash. Giant trees eventually turned to stone and flying insects and fragile flowers became locked in rock.

Clues about these extraordinary occurrences can be found around every corner at Florissant Fossil Beds National Monument. The best way to understand these ancient events is to take the 0.5-mile *Walk Through Time Nature Trail* and try to picture life and the landscape as it was during the late Eocene Epoch, about 58 to 34 million years ago.

And to understand the complete story of Florissant Fossil Beds, it helps to see the scenery west of the monument, near Guffey where an impressive ridge of darkly capped mountains, including Black Mountain, remain as evidence of the ancient volcanoes that blasted ash eastward and buried the trees and insects of Florissant Fossil Beds. Once you see these peaks, the volcanic events of Florissant fall neatly into place.

Don't Get Stumped!

The main attractions of the *Walk Through Time Nature Trail* are found only a short distance from the visitor center on Teller County 1. There are remnants of now-extinct giant redwoods that once grew three times taller than today's ponderosa pines. One prize fossil stands alone: The Big Stump is more than 41 feet around and larger than any of the mineralized trees in Petrified Forest National Park in Arizona. It looks so much like wood that it is hard to believe the massive stump is rock!

Nearby, the Trio is easy to recognize. Twelve feet high, these three trunks represent a family of ancient redwoods that sprouted from a huge parent tree. The shoots developed into full-size trees, forming a ring around the parent tree

A park ranger explains efforts to preserve petrified redwood stumps. This temporary shelter protects the Trio from deterioration by rain, snow, and ice. Metal straps around the fossils help hold them together.

after it died. Similarly, present day redwoods can be seen growing in such family circles today along the Pacific coast of Northern California.

How did these immense relics form? If you had been standing in this exact location during the late Eocene, the environment would have been much different. The average annual temperature was about 20 degrees warmer, producing a rich, nearly subtropical climate that supported hundreds of different kinds of insects and plants. And there was an active volcano nearby: About 16 miles to the southwest, not far from Guffey, a volcanic field rumbled and shook the earth for miles around.

Like Mount St. Helens in Washington in 1980, the Guffey volcanic field erupted, sending enormous mudflows directly toward the giant redwoods. Rivers of ash and mud slammed through the towering forest, wiping out many trees and surrounding others with mud up to a height of 15 feet. After the mud hardened, penetrating groundwater dissolved silica (rock crystals) in the stone and saturated the wood.This mineral solution invaded spaces between the cell walls in the buried trees and became rigid, petrifying the giant sequoias. Later eruptions sent more mudflows down the valley, sealing the petrified forest in a time capsule to be opened only after millions of years of erosion.

Farther along the *Walk Through Time Nature Trail,* a broad vista reveals a 12-mile-long valley flanked by low hills with pine woodlands. If you imagine these grassy lowlands inundated by water and, grazing along its shore, some

*The Trio was a family of living redwoods that sprouted from one
parent tree. Thirty-five million years ago, lava from a volcano snapped the
trees off to their present height of 12 feet.* National Park Service

prehistoric piglike animals or a primitive horse, you will have painted an accurate picture of ancient Lake Florissant 35 million years ago!

As the trail continues, a portion of the large prehistoric lakebed lies exposed. Paper-thin layers of this shale outcropping formed as ash and sediments from frequent volcanic eruptions were deposited in Lake Florissant. These deposits became compacted into bands of rock that today contain a wealth of precious plant and insect fossils. The expansive layer of shale was once protected by the same caprock (solidified mudflows) that covered the remains of the redwood forest. Once eroded, much of the shale also disappeared, taking with it thousands of delicate pieces of the past.

Don't be tempted to collect any of the petrified wood, fossils, or other natural or historic objects you may see! It's prohibited! Leaving these things behind helps to protect our national heritage and allows others to make discoveries, too. You may see temporary shelters over some of the stumps. The National Park Service is researching ways to preserve the petrified stumps from the effects of weather and erosion.

More Trails Through Time

• *Petrified Forest Loop*—This 1-mile hike leads across the bed of ancient Lake Florissant to one of the most stupendous petrified stumps in the world. Thirty-eight feet around and 12 feet tall, Big Stump is the highlight of any trip to Florissant Fossil Beds National Monument. Standing near the colorfully streaked megatrunk, visitors seem to be lost in thought as they look up to imagine the full height (about 300 feet) of the monstrous redwood that once stood in the ancient Eocene forest.

• *Hornbek Wildlife Loop*—Beyond Big Stump, about halfway along this 4-mile loop trail, is Hornbek Homestead; its sturdy log house, built in 1878, evokes the not-so distant past when pioneers came to the Florissant Valley. Depending on the season, you may see elk, deer, coyotes, and wildflowers.

Paleo Scene

The ancient Florissant landscape of the late Eocene featured a major stream drainage bordered by mixed hardwood forests of hickories, maples, and oaks. After the towering redwoods were entombed in volcanic mud, flows from a later eruption formed caprock that protected the petrified trees from erosion. The volcanic tuff and breccia from this eruption also dammed streams and created a lake, just like a man-made reservoir.

More than 150 species of plants and 1,200 kinds of insects lived along the shores of Lake Florissant until, over the next 500,000 years, more volcanic eruptions showered tons of ash over the region. Deadly clouds of dust caught grasshoppers, wasps, butterflies, and other insects, dragging them into the silty lake. Floating pollen, seeds, and falling leaves were caught, too, settling on the lake bottom where they were buried by sediment. Layers upon layers of fine

Powdery volcanic ash fell on this wasp millions of years ago, beginning the process of fossilization. Delicate and detailed, insect fossils from Florissant Fossil Beds are the finest in the world. National Park Service

sediments were compacted to form shale, compressing the insects and plant parts like lettuce in a sandwich. Now, when the shale is split along its natural layers, or bedding planes, delicate fossils are revealed that display details of organisms that existed nearly 35 million years ago!

Micro Scape

Most of Florissant's fossils remain hidden beneath rolling acres of wildflowers and grasslands. Only a few of the light gray fossil-bearing shales are exposed at all, and they erode very quickly in the snow, wind, and rain. The visitor center displays an impressive variety of the internationally renown fossils, providing budding paleontologists with some unforgettable close-up views.

What is so special about these particular fossils? The Florissant fossils are among the most detailed fossils in the world. Insect fossils, in particular, are uncommon, because they are so fragile. But, the powdery ash that fell on these organisms during volcanic eruptions achieved the process of preservation very gently. The volcanic caprock that later sealed the lakebed protected them as an outstanding record of the past.

In the visitor center, impressions of prehistoric caterpillars, butterflies, and beetles abound. Dark brown or black, these nearly photographic images are actually the carbon residue, or organic leftovers, of living organisms. Some of the insects are perfectly preserved: Tiny hairs and veins are even visible without a magnifying glass. Other fossils may reveal plant or insect parts: a delicate butterfly wing, a prehistoric pinecone, or tiny grains of pollen. These small-scale fossil treasures are quite a contrast to the giant fossil stumps just outside.

Back in Time Line

The first fossil collections were made in 1871, about the time a homesteader found the Big Stump while he was digging a ditch. A year later James Castello, a settler, named the nearby community Florissant, perhaps for his home town of Florissant, Missouri. It also may have been named florissant, French for "blooming," because of abundant wildflowers in the valley or the many plant fossils.

Scientists began to hear about the fossils at Florissant beginning in the 1870s. Samuel Scudder, a paleoentomologist, a scientist who studies fossil insects, collected more than 5,000 fossils in five days and wrote about them in 1873. Now at Harvard University's Museum of Comparative Zoology, in Cambridge, Massachusetts, Scudder's collection eventually amounted to 25,000 fossil insects. Since then scientists have collected more than 80,000 specimens, including several species of fish, birds, and small mammals.

Adeline Hornbek established a homestead in the valley and by 1878 had a large ranch; the ground was actually littered with pieces of petrified wood. Scientists remained the principal visitors to the valley, and tourists came by the

The historic Hornbek Homestead offers visitors a glimpse of Colorado pioneer life in the late 1800s. Here Adeline Hornbek and her four children raised horses, cattle, and poultry on their 160-acre mountain ranch.

trainload from Colorado Springs in the 1890s to collect wildflowers and see the fossils.

By 1920, much of the wood and countless fossils had been taken by tourists. Area residents and other concerned citizens realized that the fossil beds should be protected, and Florissant Fossil Beds became a national monument in August 1969 to preserve a priceless record of the past and permit visitors to continue to enjoy the area for years to come.

Travel Log

• From I-25 at Colorado Springs, take U.S. 24 35 miles west to Florissant. Turn south on Teller County 1 for 2.5 miles to the Florissant Fossil Beds Visitor Center. In good weather, the monument can be reached on graded gravel roads from Guffey, 23 miles north of Cañon City.
• At 8,300 feet in elevation, Florissant Fossil Beds is a year-round destination. Activities include hiking, horseback riding, cross-country skiing, snowshoeing, and picnicking. There are no camping facilities at the monument, but camping is available at Mueller State Park and Pike National Forest.
• The National Park Service Visitor Center at Florissant Fossil Beds is open year-round (except on winter holidays) with extended summer hours. Entrance fees are charged. For more information write: Florissant Fossil Beds National Monument, P.O. Box 185, Florissant, CO 80816.

8 Garden of the Gods

Red rocks! Carved by wind and water into spires, keyhole windows, and kissing camels—these and more geologic sculptures stir your imagination and offer an invitation to explore Colorado's most unusual city park. A beautiful jumble of monoliths, Garden of the Gods has a wilderness flavor yet amenities such as paved sidewalks (good for in-line skating), mountain bike trails, horse and hiking trails, a delightful visitor center, a trading post, historic sites, and picnic areas. From the giant slabs of glowing sandstone and the gnarled trunks of thousand-year-old junipers, this is a photographer's paradise and one of the most scenic spots in the state.

From parking lots along Ridge Road, mountain bike trails take you off the beaten path. Winding around this part of the park can be a learning experience as you explore the transition zone between the grasslands and the mountains. Pedaling up and down the slopes of these foothills, you cannot find a better backdrop for a bike ride. You'll be captivated by Cathedral Rock and the Sleeping Giant, but remember to keep your eyes peeled for other visitors for a safe trip.

A mountain biking brochure is available at the nearby visitor center, and it is a good idea to pick up a copy to be aware of regulations that protect the experience for all visitors. There is a designated bike lane on park roadways that allows bicyclists to explore much more of the park. Remember, safety gear is essential equipment.

The *Gateway Trail* is paved, and combined with the *Central Garden Trail*, this 2-mile loop launches hikers right into and around many of the rock formations. This route is perfect for visitors with strollers or other special needs. Both of these trails are found smack in the heart of the 2-square-mile park and provide you with the experience of being surrounded by the gigantic slabs of stone.

Whether you choose to stroll, bike, or hike in the park, the rocks remain the main attraction. Even though each towering slab bears a name listed on park maps, invent your own names. Like watching clouds, you may see animal shapes in the stone or profiles of people. Shapes must really have impressed early visitors who named Pulpit Rock, Scotsman, Siamese Twins, Steamboat

A visit to the Garden of the Gods is like wandering through a maze of natural wonders. The early morning sun lights up Gateway and Cathedral Rocks as if they were on fire.

Rock, Toad and Toadstools, and Sleeping Giant. Search for your own portraits in stone, though. There are plenty of opportunities for you to find some curious figure that you can name!

Paleo Scene

Beyond the eastward-stretching shadows of Pikes Peak, final rays of sunshine highlight eroded sandstone sediments tilted up by forces of mountain building during the last 75 million years. When you look into the Garden of the Gods from the east, you see colorful pages of geologic history tipped up for you to read like a book. The first chapter that you encounter from Gateway Road, is the youngest. Propped up here is a hogback of white sandstone that formed during the Jurassic period, between 135 to 200 million years ago. Behind the chalky slabs of White and Cathedral Rocks, a red layer of Triassic shale, a little softer than the sandstone, ranges from 200 to 240 million years old.

On *Gateway Trail*, you hike between two massive sentinels of sandstone from the Permian Period, North and South Gateway Rocks. These monumental blades of peach-colored stone are very resistant to weathering. Geologists suggest that individual sand grains in this layer are cemented together with silica and a mineral called hematite that creates a hard bond and produces the unforgettable salmon hues in the park.

On the west side of Garden of the Gods, Pennsylvanian age shales from 280 to 325 million years ago are not quite so vertically arranged. Darker red and occasionally banded with a rough pebbly conglomerate (a mixture of sand and larger sized rounded pebbles of older rock), this layer erodes into mushroom-shaped formations, with occasional balanced rocks. These teetering giants form when more weather-resistant rocks remain after the softer layer of rock below has eroded away, leaving the upper rocks to an unsteady future. Check out the peculiar formations along Garden Drive. Can you predict the fate of the Siamese Twins or Balanced Rock?

While you hike, bike, or ride on horseback through the park look for the smaller details of geologic history, too. Ripple marks in sandstone may have been left in a small prehistoric lake. In some formations, bands of small rounded pebbles reveal a stream environment, where rocks once tumbled along in currents, rounding off their edges. Search for tiny mud cracks, now solid stone in the shale layers that indicate a wet period followed by drought that caused the mud to crack.

Micro Scape

Without its piñon pine and juniper woodlands, Garden of the Gods would look a lot more like another planet! Dotting the crimson landscape with deep specks of green, these short, shrubby conifers make up a pygmy forest.

Common where soils are shallow and poor in nutrients, these stubby trees seem to sprout from solid rock! Look up on some of the tallest formations and try to figure out how these plants grow. How did they get there in the first place?

Wind may have played a part, but likely seeds dropped by birds fell into rock crevices where just enough erosion occured to create some soil. Somewhat protected from wind and weather, the seeds sprouted, and the tree's woody roots penetrated cracks seeking moisture, and now stubbornly cling to life, growing into works of art shaped by strong winds, hundreds of feet above the ground!

Back in Time Line

Garden of the Gods contains a human landscape that begins with Indian legends. These first Americans saw the rock formations as the remains of animals drowned in a great flood and turned to stone. Ancestors of the Cheyenne, Arapaho, and Ute often camped among the rocks and gathered fruits like chokecherries and piñon pine nuts. They also killed elk and buffalo that they had driven into box canyons and narrow passes.

The Gateway Trail leads visitors into the heart of the Garden of the Gods rock formations. The Kissing Camels are just around the bend!

Once horizontal, the layers of red sandstone in Garden of the Gods have been tilted nearly vertical. In 1890, early visitors came by horse and buggy to marvel at the dramatic formations carved by wind and water erosion.
Colorado Historical Society

From the first visitors, Garden of the Gods attracted a procession of visitors: explorers and gold seekers, settlers and entrepreneurs. Look for signs of their impact on the garden. Some are subtle, others are bold.

Timeless Traces of Early Travels

Along the *Gateway Trail*, look for rock formations that bear inscriptions made by early travelers. The first gold seekers carved their names into the rock walls in 1858 to document their stay. Later visitors added their names and dates.

Be respectful of the spirit of the great explorers found on these walls. When you consider the need to leave evidence of our passing through new and dangerous territory, remember that modern visits to Garden of the Gods cannot compare to the hazards overcome by early pioneers. It is important to protect the historic record, and additions are illegal. This way, future generations can wonder about the obstacles courageous people defeated to reach new places.

The park's name originiated in 1859 when a settler had a notion that the area would make a great beer garden! Believing the site was suitable enough for "the Gods to assemble," his partner proposed that it was more appropriate to call it a "Garden of the Gods," and the name stuck. These two resourceful pioneers, Melancthon Beach and Rufus Cable, founded nearby Colorado City, named Colorado, Spanish for red, because of the area's red rock formations. You can visit the site of old Colorado City just northwest of the junction of U.S. 24 and Interstate 25.

Also take time to explore the Rock Ledge Ranch Historic Site to witness living history presentations. In summer, interesting programs re-create lifestyles and conditions on the nineteenth-century ranch. This presents a special opportunity to step back in time and see how the game of baseball was played in the late 1800s, or how horse-drawn equipment was operated. Rather than just quaint activities and unusual artifacts, the ranch offers visitors a chance to compare the daily routines of an earlier era with today's lifestyle. You will discover that the basic pursuits of making a living, being comfortable, and seeking fun remain the same.

Travel Log

•   Garden of the Gods is west of Colorado Springs. Take the Garden of the Gods Road (Exit 147) from Interstate 25 and follow the signs. If you are coming from Woodland Park or Manitou Springs on U.S. 24, exit on Manitou Avenue and follow Garden of the Gods signs to the Balanced Rock entrance.

•   There is no admission fee. The park was a gift to Colorado Springs by Charles Elliot Perkins who died in 1907. His heirs specified that there be no charge, when the land was finally transferred to the city in 1909. A visitor center on the east side of the park on 30th Street is a great place to begin your exploration.

•   Technical rock climbers must register at the visitor center; scrambling and sport rappelling are prohibited.

9
Glenwood Canyon

Discovery Zone

Just west of Dotsero, Interstate 70 enters an incredibly scenic 12-mile stretch of fun, adventure, and discovery. For millions of years, the Colorado River has been carving a canyon through here. Roaring with wild rapids in some places and snaking smoothly along in others, this westward flowing ribbon of water begs to be explored. There are so many opportunities packed into this narrow canyon that it may be tough to pick a place to start!

An Artery of Adventure

You wouldn't normally think of a highway as a place to play, but this stretch of road will change your mind! Enormous care and planning went into building this major east-west highway that carries millions of cars and trucks each year.

Not far from the busy highway, gardens and lakes offer drivers and their passengers a chance to get out of their cars to enjoy slow-paced walks in amazingly accessible natural settings. A paved bike trail follows the river the entire length of the canyon, from which you glimpse whitewater rapids before river rafters even know what to expect! Another point of interest along the road is an historic electric power plant that operates under the suspended highway where a viaduct, or bridge, carries the roadbed within inches of the canyon walls.

The town of Glenwood Springs, at the western mouth of the canyon, is renown for having the world's largest outdoor hot springs pool that encourages relaxation in summer and winter. These natural hot springs were first visited by Ute Indians who believed the waters could cure illness, and they called them Yampa Springs, meaning Big Medicine.

Many famous people have stayed at what has come to be known as Colorado's Spa in the Rockies, including President Theodore Roosevelt. Over the years, developers have constructed two swimming pools with areas for sunning and relaxing in the shade. Not so small at all, the small pool is 100 feet long, and the large pool is 405 feet long and 100 feet wide. Water temperatures for the large, million-gallon pool at Glenwood Hot Springs reach 90° F; the small pool stays at about 104°. On a winter evening clouds of steam rise from the surface of the warm pool to mix with cold air to add a special pleasure to wading in the warm waters.

At the Hanging Lake Exit, Interstate 70 threads through delicate ecosystems, hangs from steep canyon walls, and dips near the edge of the Colorado River. A bike path winds along the highway through Glenwood Canyon.

Crypto Scene

Now this is a real hideaway! On the interstate, midway through the Hanging Lake Tunnel, is an underground control center that looks like Mission Control for the space program. Here a staff monitors traffic and trouble spots along the 12-mile stretch of highway through the canyon, especially in the tunnel, using remote television cameras. The center receives up-to-the-minute reports from weather stations along the highway, so that operators can alert motorists of safe speeds or blocked lanes. There are also sensors in the tunnel roadway that report stalled vehicles or slow moving traffic; and there are heat detectors that can report vehicle fires. If operators need to communicate emergency information to motorists, they use a radio system that broadcasts on your car radio, regardless of the station you are tuned to, to instruct drivers how to avoid trouble.

The beauty of Glenwood Canyon can be enjoyed from the paved bike path that winds between the river and the highway. Numerous rest stops along the path are great stops for a picnic and a chance to watch river rafters.

Micro Scape

The natural environment within the canyon is an extra bonus for through travelers. The Colorado River attracts bighorn sheep, mule deer, and even an occasional cougar. Take time to walk or bike along the river, or take the short hike to Hanging Lake.

• *Hanging Lake Trail*—To find Hanging Lake from the east, take the Grizzly Creek exit and turn around to Exit 125 (there is only a west-bound exit). The trailhead, at the east end of the rest area parking lot, climbs 1,000 feet in 1 mile, and the round trip takes about 2 hours.

Hanging Lake was created when the floor of the lakebed broke off along a fault line in the long valley above. Travertine deposits (calcium carbonate in the water) built up where the water spilled over the broken edge, creating a small dam. A waterfall below Hanging Lake and spray from the Spouting Rock just above the falls offer welcome relief from summer heat.

Plan to spend at least 30 minutes at the lake, and listen for a canyon wren whose descending notes echo off the canyon walls.

Indians and early explorers chose not to use the canyon as a thoroughfare because it was too rugged. Nineteenth century railroad builders, however, blasted a narrow-gauge route through the canyon in 1887. It was later widened to standard gauge. In 1890, a primitive stagecoach road was built, and by 1900 an automobile road. Barney Oldfield roared through the canyon on the dirt road during a 1906 coast-to-coast automobile race.

Glenwood Canyon's beauty inspired the idea for the modern-day Vista Dome cars on passenger trains. A General Motors vice-president who was testing a freight locomotive through the canyon, thought that people would pay good money to enjoy the scenery as much as he had. He sketched a glass-domed car, an idea that eventually led to the observation cars of the famed California and Denver Zephyr of the Denver & Rio Grande Western Railroad. Today, Amtrak passengers enjoy the same view.

To Build or Not to Build?

The construction of this road marks a significant point in the environmental movement because citizens worked together to protect the nature of the canyon. They were concerned that upgrading the two-lane road to a modern

The sandstone castle serves as a clubhouse for the million-gallon Glenwood Hot Springs pool at the western end of Glenwood Canyon. The warm water is a great retreat from the cold air in winter or a relaxing end to a long bike ride.

four-lane interstate would be too destructive. Their persistent care ensured that the design approach for Glenwood Canyon would be different.

It took more than 20 years from the initial request to build the multilane highway through Glenwood Canyon until the final design was agreed upon and approved. It took 12 more years to actually construct it. And it was finally completed in 1993 at a cost of $450 million.

Building the highway meant resolving conflicting demands. Project engineers had to solve how to increase traffic capacity on the old road, improve safety, construct a road that would not damage the fragile beauty of the canyon, and confine contruction to previously disturbed ground. What a tall order in such a narrow canyon!

Full-scale mock-ups of bridge-support structures were built in place so that the public could weigh the visual and environmental impacts of the system. A special piece of equipment had to be designed and built to construct the many bridges or viaducts. Artists created numerous sketches of the roadway, as it would appear from the driver's seat of a car driving on the yet-to-be-built highway, as well as drawings of what the highway would look like from across the canyon.

Revegetation was carefully planned. Specific plant lists were developed for canyon walls, roadside areas, and the riverbank. Native species were identified and planted, and a watering system ensured that the new plants would survive. More than 150,000 native plants were eventually used to eliminate construction scars, and care was also taken to reduce the damage done to existing plants. Penalties were charged for destruction: Destroy a raspberry bush and the fine was $30; kill a scrub oak, $45; cut down a blue spruce, Colorado's state tree, and it would cost the construction company $2,200!

While you travel through the canyon, study the rock walls carefully. Where blasting took place, landscape architects studied adjacent cliffs and directed work crews to sculpture the blasted surfaces to look like the surrounding rocks. Where there was desert varnish, a mineral stain, on the canyon walls, workers painted or stained blasted walls with a solution of mild acid, dissolved manganese, and iron oxide to match it.

On the Road Again

The last stages of construction activity in the canyon resulted in some extraordinary approaches to road building. To minimize environmental disturbances, the road was suspended above the ground in some places. A special overhead gantry was imported from France to accomplish this. Sections of viaducts and bridges were precast in concrete and trucked in and lifted in place by crane. These 100,000-pound sections were connected to each other like Tinker Toys and gradually filled the gaps between vertical pylons that held the road above the ground. The crane moved along the completed sections of the road as it was finished, virtually building the road for itself, not needing to touch or disturb the ground between the pylons.

You may notice that the roadway is often wider than the base upon which it is built. In fact, the road overhangs its foundations by up to six feet on each side. This allowed the east and west lanes to be built much closer together and reduced the area that needed to be disturbed in order to build the road. The retaining walls that needed to be built to support the road had to be up to 40 feet high in some places. But this visual intrusion was minimized because shadows created by the overhanging road keeps part of the retaining wall in the dark, creating the illusion of a smaller wall!

Travel Log

• Bring a picnic to enjoy at one of the many rest stops along the interstate as well as bikes so you can pedal along the Colorado River on the paved bike path. You can rent bikes in Glenwood Springs, and the bike path is excellent for in-line skating, too.
• Rafting and kayaking are tremendously popular here and guide services are listed in local directories.
• Glenwood Hot Springs, (970) 945-7131, and Yampah Vapor Caves, (970) 945-0667, are open seven days a week with changing rooms and shower facilities for pool guests. Admission fees are charged.

Hang on! Though mild by untamed river standards, a raft trip through Glenwood Canyon offers plenty of thrills, especially on an all-day trip, which begins at the eastern end of the canyon. Prepare to get wet!

10
Great Sand Dunes National Monument

Discovery Zone

Nestled next to the rugged and spectacular Sangre de Cristo Mountains, Great Sand Dunes National Monument is an uncommon place for an un-ordinary exploration experience. Rising more than 700 feet above the San Luis Valley, the tallest sand dunes in North America cover an area of 39 square miles. Combine these enormous piles of sand with lots of sun and a sense of discovery, and plenty of thrills are bound to result.

Who needs snow?

You won't be able to resist sliding down these mammoth mountains of sand—no matter what your age. Snowboards, skis, plastic sleds—you name it; if you can carry it to the top, you can use it to get down. Hang-gliders are the only equipment prohibited on the dunes, due to unsafe wind conditions.

The best destination for a quick skid down the dunes is directly north and west of the visitor center on Colorado 150. No trails stay on the dunes for long, so just head for the highest point. Be sure to wear shoes and take plenty of water; in summer, the temperature of the sand can reach 140°F,

Climbing up the dunes is tough work, but the return trip is loads of fun. From the top of any dune you can slide, tumble, run, or jump off into midair. There is no closer feeling to flying, and the landing is generally soft. Conditions on the dunes are often windy and hot, so wear sunglasses and footwear for protection.

The natural condition of the main dune mass is protected as a wilderness to offer visitors a primitive experience away from motorized vehicles.

making both items a must. It's about 1.0 mile to the highest point on the dunes, and the hike is easier if you climb in a zigzag fashion. Following the ridges to the top makes the walk less of a grind and takes no more time than a direct route.

The panorama from the top of the dunes is one of the greatest in Colorado. Far to the west you can see the 14,000-foot San Juan Mountains, headwaters of the Rio Grande. Most of the sand deposited at the dunes comes from the San Juans. Try to trace the route of Medano Creek as it flows along the bottom of the steep eastern dunes before heading southwest to disappear into the sand.

You'll also glimpse Escape Dunes and Ghost Forest. Shifting sands from the main dunes cross Medano Creek at this point, forming new dunes that are covering up vegetation and creating ghost forests where sand suffocates tall ponderosa pines.

The round-trip to the top of the dunes and back takes less than two hours. Snowboarders, skiers, and other serious sliders can descend in a hurry. Be aware of hikers and thrill seekers on the way down. Collisions can hurt, even on tons of soft sand!

One of the wildest thrills on the dunes is simply to jump off. You can feel as if you're flying when you leap off a 700-foot sand dune. Visitors get hooked on this experience and climb up again and again to vault, leap, hurdle, and bound back to earth. This is the ultimate experience of any visit to the dunes.

Fishing, hiking, horseback riding, and four-wheeling are other activities in and around Great Sand Dunes National Monument. Be aware that regulations differ on National Park Service lands and nearby United States Forest Service lands. For instance, no motorized equipment is allowed in the main dune wilderness to preserve its natural condition. However, four-wheel-drive vehicles are permitted along Medano Road, on the east side of the monument, and in certain areas of the Rio Grande National Forest. Check out these other activities that range from a stroll through a cool forest to a wild ride over Medano Pass.

Paleo Scene

Nearly 12,000 years of continual motion have shaped the dramatic dunes of this national monument. Why are these dunes so far from any desert or ocean? Three elements essential to dune formation combine at this unique location. Sand, wind, and a sheltered place make this a classic site for nature to create such an outstanding attraction.

Millions of years ago, the San Luis Valley stayed in place when the earth's crust gradually lifted the Rockies 5,000 feet. The valley remained part of a low-lying region bordered by faults that elevated the volcanic San Juan Mountains to the west and the Sangre de Cristos to the east. As glaciers bull-dozed rocks and soil from the mountain ranges, layers of sand, silt, gravel, and volcanic debris carried by the Rio Grande accumulated in the broad valley.

Many years later, the climate warmed and the San Luis Valley became too dry for many plants to survive. Without protective vegetation, valley soils were exposed to the elements. Wind carried sand particles away to the northeast toward the Sangre de Cristo Mountains. The mountain barrier formed a pocket where grains of sand could only escape up through a few glacier-carved passes. Rising winds dropped most of the heavy sand, carrying only a little dust beyond the Sangre de Cristos. Deposits eventually accumulated into impressive mountains of sand.

This process, over thousands of years, formed the incredible dunes that are still changing today. Most of the sand you see is composed of dark volcanic rock from as far away as the San Juan Mountains, deposited by way of the Rio Grande. Very little of the sand in the dunes comes from the lighter minerals in the Sangre de Cristos. That is why these formations have a darker appearance than most other dunes. Rather than reflecting light as lighter-colored sand

Powerful winds pick up sand from the San Luis Valley and carry the grains toward the Sangre de Cristo Mountains. Much of the sand fun-nels into an indentation in the range and bounces around in air currents before falling to the bottom of mountain passes. National Park Service

Glassy clumps of fused sand called
fulgurites are sometimes found on
the dunes. These oddly shaped
rocks form when lightning strikes a
dune and welds sand grains together
with intense heat.

National Park Service

particles do, these dunes absorb light and retain more heat. Great solar radiation collectors, the dunes become very hot in summer, keeping hikers from going barefoot.

You can learn about sand dunes. Identify types of dunes and guess how they are formed. Reversing dunes and star dunes are created where the wind whips around in many directions. These dunes have steep downwind slopes or slipfaces on all sides. Linear or transverse dunes and crescent-shaped barchan dunes have gentle upwind sides and steep downwind sides. Winds blow sand grains from the gentle side to the slipface causing the dunes to creep. The eastern edge of the main dune mass is shaped by these very steep dunes, making them a great jumping off point for dune adventures!

Approaching storms are often accompanied by lightning that may strike the highest point around. When lightning hits, sand particles fuse or melt together, creating a fulgurite. Often glassy and tubular, fulgurites are a rare find on the dunes, so leave them for others to discover. Remember, too, that lightning is a danger if you are high on the dunes. If storm clouds arise, come down off the dunes or return to the safety of your vehicle.

Crypto Scene

When you visit Great Sand Dunes, investigate mysterious Medano Creek. This is an opportunity to solve one of the greatest natural puzzles in Colorado! Flowing at its highest in May and June, this cold, shallow creek pulsates with an irregular rhythm almost like ocean waves. And if that isn't strange enough, the water actually vanishes into the sand at the southern end of the dunes!

Most people stop abruptly when this happens: At one moment, the water is calm with a flat surface. Seconds later, the creek surges along in small rippling waves that suddenly stop—as if on command from some unseen force.

This mystery prompted researchers to study the pulsating movement of Medano Creek. They discovered that certain conditions in the streambed determine how fast the water flows. Water travels at a high speed where the sandy bottom of the stream channel is smooth. In some areas of the creek, symmetrical mounds of sand (like ripples) accumulate underwater. These "antidunes" slow the water as it moves up and down over their sandy surfaces. As a result, 20 percent more water is stored in the creek where antidunes occur. When these mounds of sand collapse, the water surges in a wave and accelerates along the stream channel until another bed of antidunes causes the cycle to repeat.

Throughout this cycle of surging stream flow, Medano Creek slowly sinks into the sand. Sand particles actually capture water along the entire course of the creek, transferring it to an underground storage area. This huge layer of water-soaked gravel below the dunes is called an aquifer. By the time Medano Creek flows southwest past the visitor center, it has completely disappeared, depositing all of its water into the aquifer beneath the shifting dunes. Some of this water reappears west of Great Sand Dunes National Monument at San Luis Lake, the lowest point in the San Luis Valley.

Scientists monitor the upper level, or water table, of the aquifer. In some areas of the San Luis Valley, the water table has dropped significantly in recent times. Studies may show this is due to overall changes in the climate or because of irrigation for farms and ranches.

Water plays an important role in dune stability. Geologists believe that the dunes mostly remain in place because they are moist throughout. Water from rain and snow moves past surface sand particles that stay dry and move freely in the wind. Much of the water remains in the sand dunes before it slowly flows underground. So, dunes that appear hot and dry on the surface, may be cool and moist only inches below!

Medano Creek borders the eastern edge of the dunes and provides a refreshing place to splash around on a hot summer day. Water from the creek disappears completely into the sand just downstream.

Wild Things

Neither rats nor kangaroos, kangaroo rats are actually members of the mouse family. They hop like kangaroos on their hind legs, holding their front paws close to their bodies. These quick little rodents use their long tails for balance, leaving unmistakable tracks where they hop on the dunes. Kangaroo rats have special fur-lined pockets on either side of their mouths for storing the seeds and blades of grass they gather at night. Specially adapted to arid climate, kangaroo rats never have to drink water. Their food contains all the water they need!

Organisms including this kangaroo rat have special adaptations to survive desert life. The rodent is active only at night and drinks no water. It obtains moisture in this arid habitat from the seeds it eats.

National Park Service

Relatives of the kangaroo rat, deer mice prefer to remain hidden among grasses and shrubs. They dart out in the open to find berries, seeds, fruits, and insects, but quickly retreat when predators are present. Their small, white feet leave delicate imprints that often tell the tale of a hunt in the night.

Both predators and prey make up a colorful cast of characters at Great Sand Dunes. Some of the most hunted animals are cottontail rabbits, distinguished from jackrabbits by their smaller size and cotton ball tails. Although it is a great sprinter, a cottontail has only a 1 in 20 chance of reaching its first birthday due to predation. Sometimes you may see cottontail tracks end in a blur where a predator has won a scuffle.

One of the hunters on the dunes is the bobcat, named for its short, stubby tail. Very secretive, bobcats are rarely seen. At night, they hunt for rabbits, squirrels, chipmunks, and sometimes deer. During the day, they rest in dens of shrubs next to the dunes.

Micro Scape

Some living things can be found at Great Sand Dunes that exist nowhere else in the world. Why? Because conditions on the dunes are extreme. This environment can be very hot, dry, and windy in summer and cold and snowy during winter.

Giant sand treader camel crickets are one of three species of dune insects that occur nowhere else in the world. The cricket's fringed hind feet work like baskets to scoop sand out of its burrows.

National Park Service

Dune Buggies

A few especially unusual insects live only in this area. Great Sand Dunes tiger beetles are active, fast-running, and quick-flying. Their metallic, patterned bodies scurry along the dunes in search of other insects to prey on. Careful inspection of tiny sand tunnels may reveal tiger beetle larvae waiting to capture passing insects. Their bite can be quite painful, so observation is best from a distance.

Circus beetles live in the grassland and piñon-juniper forest as well as on the dunes. Dull and black, these tiny acrobats protect themselves from predators using a special talent. They tilt their back-ends up at an angle and spray a foul-smelling black fluid in the direction of any threat. Only one predator is known to resist this tactic—the grasshopper mouse.

Equipped with special tools to navigate the sand, giant sand treader camel crickets are normally active at night. These large, hump-backed insects have a sort of fringe around their feet that looks like baggy socks. These structures act like baskets for shoveling sand out of newly constructed burrows. Sightings of camel crickets and tiger beetles should be reported at the visitor center to assist in research about these insects.

Plants in the Sand

Blowout grass, scurfpea, Indian ricegrass, and prairie sunflowers have adapted to the harsh, windy conditions of the dunes. Special leaf surfaces, stems, and roots help these plants resist water loss. Moist sand below the surface provides water for these plants to produce seeds that are a valuable source of food for birds and rodents. Imagine how you would change your lifestyle to adapt to the unique environment of the dunes.

Back in Time Line

Spanish explorers traveled here in the 1600s to seek gold, adventure, and religious converts. One story tells of a Spanish priest who was fatally wounded in a battle with Indians. Just before he died, he saw the mountains to the east burning red at sunset. He gasped, "Sangre de Cristo!" (Blood of Christ), thus naming the mountain range with his last breath.

Hike into History

• *Mosca Pass Trail*—If you traveled over Mosca Pass in 1871, you would have paid a gatekeeper to get to the other side! This toll road was once a busy route for travelers on their way to the San Luis Valley. Washed out during a flash flood in 1906, the road was no longer needed when a railroad was built to the south. This 7-mile round-trip hike gains 1,463 feet in elevation as it meanders through piñon-juniper, aspen, and spruce-fir forests. The meadows at the top welcome hikers to rest, enjoy lunch, and watch for wildlife. Bears may be seen here, as well as deer and a variety of birds.

• *Wellington Ditch Trail*—Named Wellington for a homesteader who settled here in the 1920s, this 2-mile round-trip trail follows an irrigation ditch from the *Montville Nature Trail* to Piñon Flats Campground. Wellington hand-dug the mile-long ditch to carry water from Mosca Creek to his homestead near Piñon Flats. As you hike along this route, notice that parts of the trail follow the original ditch.

Travel Log

• For information write: Great Sand Dunes National Monument, 11500 Colorado 150, Mosca, CO 81146. Stop by the visitor center, open year-round except on Christmas Day, to check current conditions before you venture into the dunes. Exhibits and publications are available, as well as assistance from rangers and volunteers. Some activities such as guided hikes and campfire programs are available during summer.

• Piñon Flats Campground is open all year without reservations. Backcountry camping at designated sites requires a permit. Open fires and wood gathering are prohibited. Picnic areas are available.

• In summer, take sunscreen, a hat, sunglasses, shoes for walking on hot sand, and plenty of water. At an average elevation of about 8,000 feet, the weather at Great Sand Dunes is generally mild, but temperatures on the dunes can reach 140°F. In winter, temperatures can fall below freezing.

Four-wheeling on Medano Road is a wild ride for those exploring the eastern edge of the monument. Thrills range from deep ruts in the sand to splashes through muddy puddles on the way to Medano Pass.

11 Little Bookcliffs Wild Horse Area

When the dewy morning quiet of the Little Bookcliffs near Grand Junction is broken by a soft snort or a playful nicker, wildlife watchers catch their breath and move in slow motion. Patience is of the utmost importance. Stillness is required. Each tiny sound seems unbearably magnified. Even the slightest cracking of a branch makes hearts skip because everyone wants to spy a band of wild horses that must be just out of sight.

Only eight miles as a crow flies north of Grand Junction, is the rugged 34,000-acre Little Bookcliffs Wild Horse Area. About two-thirds of the area, ranging in elevation from 5,000 to 7,421 feet, is covered by piñon and juniper woodlands, while badlands, canyons, plateaus, and sage make up the rest of mustang country.

Signs of the 80 or more roaming mustangs are just about as numerous as the pesky gnats that swarm the area in the warmer months: Under piñon and junipers, bright red Indian paintbrush lie flattened by hooves, and a maze of dusty paths snake in and out of the sagebrush. Welcome breezes from the valley below sweep over the dirt littered by dried manure, and hundreds of hoofprints are stamped on the plateau's roads, making this place look like a wild horse superhighway!

The best way to see the wild horses is to live with them, or at least camp where they live. There are no improved campground facilities within the Wild Horse Area boundaries, but you may camp throughout the area, and overnight camping is the best way to see the mustangs.

Cool evenings and brisk dawns mean action at Little Bookcliffs. With tents set up, campers settle down to view some interesting equine activities at dusk. Luck is the only certainty involved in spotting the wild horses. Some people may visit late in the day for only an hour or two and see mustangs trotting from meadow to meadow. Others may stay overnight and catch only a glimpse of a buckskin. Either way, the anticipation of seeing a bold stallion galloping across the mesa will undoubtedly fill your soul with the timeless spirit of the Old West, making the trip worthwhile.

So, how can you see the horses? Serious wild-horse watchers may be awakened at sunrise by the sounds of fighting stallions or stomping hooves. Daybreak is a good time to observe horses grazing or making their way to one

A young paint stallion guards his band of wild horses along the road to Monument Rocks. Curious mustangs may try to approach visitors, but the protective studs often stop such encounters. Marty Felix

of the watering holes along the mesa. But the summer sun rises high and hot over the Wild Horse Area, making viewing hours short for most horse-watchers. By midmorning, the skittish mix of bay, sorrel, black, and other beauties retreats to shade until twilight.

Crypto Scene

Many people do not know that wild horses still roam the ranges of the United States. Even fewer people know that some of these horses can be adopted! But why are wild horses sometimes gathered for adoption?

Bureau of Land Management range managers keep a close eye on the condition of horses and the vegetation in the Wild Horse Area. With the birth of foals in spring, herd numbers may increase up to 20 percent each year. Although mustangs are occasionally preyed on by cougars, only a few die from complications when trying to give birth or from breaking a leg and becoming unable to forage. In addition, dry years mean there is less vegetation for horses to eat. So, there are a lot of horses living where there is only so much food to go around. Each spring, the mustangs are counted and if the range is suffering from too many horses, some may be collected for adoption. Without intermittent roundups for adoptions, more animals might die or face starvation.

Bureau of Land Management roundups are held occasionally to keep wild horse populations in check. Mustangs captured through the Adopt-A-Wild Horse or Burro Program acquire new homes with qualified potential owners. Grand Junction resident Jared Welsh cares for an adopted Bookcliffs mare named Alyeska. Jared thinks that with time, training, and patience, adopted mustangs make excellent riding horses as well as good companions.

Adopt a Horse; Adopt a Burro!

How can you adopt a wild horse or burro? Parents, guardians, or anyone over the age of 18 may complete an application to qualify for wild horse ownership. A potential owner must also have the finances and facilities to provide humane care and treatment for any adopted animal. Once adopted, each animal is marked with a special freeze brand that identifies it as an adopted wild horse. Many mustangs can become affectionate family or ranch horses given time, patience, and proper training. For more information on the Adopt-A-Wild Horse or Burro Program, contact the Bureau of Land Management's Royal Gorge Resource Area, P.O. Box 2200, Cañon City, CO 81215-2200.

Wild Things

Wild horses range the Little Bookcliffs in bands, or small family groups. The robust boss of a band is the dominant stallion, or stud, that protects his harem of two or three mares and young offspring from danger. Sensing peril, the stallion orders his band to flee. The stud then checks out the hazard and issues a warning to any intruder before rejoining his band. If the trespasser happens to be another stallion, a fight may follow. Squeals, snorts, bites, and kicks often resolve such territorial disputes. Studs mark their domain with heaps of manure called stud piles. Drivers should dodge these natural markers on the road, leaving the piles to serve their purpose and allow other visitors an unusual sight!

Gallant stallions settle a territorial dispute in Coal Canyon. Studs kick and bite during their fights to establish dominance. The victor protects a harem of mares and their offspring from threats such as predators and people. Marty Felix

Mares also take their turn as guides through the sagebrush. Lead mares, second-in-command to dominant stallions, direct the band to grazing areas and watering holes.

What do the horses graze on? Although forage appears sparse much of the year, the mares know that stout native grasses such as Indian ricegrass, western wheatgrass, needle-and-thread, and wild rye provide a lot of nutrition. Wild horses may even nip the scrubby leaves of Gamble oaks for additional nutrients. In summer, if food becomes particularly scarce, horses nibble on sagebrush to supplement their diets. But in spring, when mares drop their foals, food is plentiful.

At age two young stallions are driven from their maternal band by the boss stallions. Abandoned, the inexperienced horses follow the band at a distance until they encounter other male horses and form a group of their own. These bachelor bands are made up of old stallions that have lost their mares and stallions that have none. Such bachelor horses often tag along with family bands, because most wild horses are very social animals.

While the wild horses seem friendly, they are really shy and cautious. Although foals romp and frolic around their mothers, they must learn to survive predators such as coyotes and mountain lions. When danger threatens, most wild horses run away, but a stallion may stand his ground and aggressively defend his territory from intruders—including dogs and people. Remember, careful wild horse-watchers observe from a distance.

Back in Time Line

More than 10,000 years ago, small, prehistoric horses lived in some parts of Colorado, roaming freely much like mule deer do today. However, no evidence of the horses remained after the last ice age. Many centuries later, in the 1500s, Spanish explorers reintroduced horses, mustaños, to North America. American Indians gradually acquired horses, and European settlers who moved west brought their own animals to work on farms and ranches.

Over the years, some of the horses strayed or were turned loose, setting the stage for populations of wild horses, or mustangs. In some areas, wild horses shared the range with burros abandoned by prospectors. Most of the Little Bookcliffs horses are probably descendants of local ranch, farming, or mining stock set free in the early 1900s. Evidence suggests that some of the wild horses may be related to Indian ponies that lived in the Bookcliffs before ranchers arrived.

Friends of the Mustangs

Why do the mustangs need protection? As wild horse populations increased in California, Nevada, Montana, Wyoming, and other states, the human population of the West also grew. Some settlers regarded wild mustangs and burros as pests and hunted them until their numbers were drastically reduced.

By the 1950s, there was public concern for the welfare of the horses and burros. Velma B. "Wild Horse Annie" Johnston of Reno, Nevada, led a crusade to protect wild horses and burros nationwide. Passed in 1959, the Wild Horse Annie Act made thousands of Americans aware of the threats to wild horses and burros. Her efforts, along with the work of many school-age children writing to members of Congress, resulted in the Wild Free-Roaming Horse and Burro Act of 1971. This law led to the establishment of the Little Bookcliffs Wild Horse Area, one of three wild horse ranges in the United States.

Today, visitors to the Bookcliffs can stop near the entrance to Indian Park off Winter Flats Road and see a monument dedicated to Wild Horse Annie. Although the Bureau of Land Management now protects the wild horse herds, private citizens still carry on Velma B. Johnston's legacy through volunteer work. By maintaining range improvements, clearing watering holes, and assisting with roundups and adoptions, volunteers have become the mustangs best friends.

Marty Felix, a full-time schoolteacher, otherwise known as the "Bookcliff Wild Horse Lady," has spent an average of 300 hours a year for 24 years working as a volunteer at the Little Bookcliffs Wild Horse Area. She is so drawn to the horses that she sometimes spends whole days photographing them. "I always feel like an honorary harem member," she says when she sees bands. "If the band seems skittish and threatened, I apologize to them for the intrusion and move on, thrilled that I was at least fortunate enough to catch a glimpse of them, no matter how brief the encounter."

Travel Log

• Camping, horseback riding, biking, and hiking are permitted throughout the Wild Horse Area, but consideration of the mustangs comes first. Vehicles must stay on established roads to protect soils and vegetation. Low-impact camping (100 feet away from any water source) is recommended. All areas are undeveloped: There is no drinking water, and no waste, or disposal facilities. Take food, two gallons of water per person per day, warm clothes, sunscreen, and a hat. Camp stoves are the best way to cook in order to minimize fire

Weird badlands called the Goblins rise up alongside South Dry Fork Road like gnomes guarding the route to Indian Park. This is a good place to pause and inspect some features called hoodoos that are the result of erosion.

hazards and preserve woodlands. Pets should be leashed to keep them from disturbing the wild horses.

Rough country, the Little Bookcliffs Wild Horse Area is not easy to reach. High clearance vehicles are necessary to negotiate winding clay roads that are impassable in wet weather. Dry days from late spring through fall are recommended; have plenty of fuel and a good spare tire.

•   *Coal Canyon Trailhead*—A few miles northwest of Cameo, off Interstate 70, lies the Coal Canyon Trailhead. From this point, beginning mountain horse riders and hikers can explore Coal Canyon and Main Canyon, winter havens for wild mustangs. The gate in Coal Canyon is open June through November for vehicles to venture part of the way. This area is closed from December through May for foaling season.

•   Dry Fork Road—This four-wheel-drive route requires commitment and a whole day or overnight visit. From DeBeque, just north of Interstate 70, the paved Roan Creek Road is marked with small brown signs to the Wild Horse Area. A tricky intersection near ranch land points north and west to Dry Fork Road. Take Dry Fork Road west, following the *Wild Horse Trail* markers through cattle country. Look for weirdly sculpted badlands once the road starts to climb up a plateau. This is a great place to rest and take photographs of the Goblins, rock formations eroded from the Bookcliffs shale. At the edge of the woodlands on the north side of the road lies a panoramic view of more badlands, including a small rock arch. After about 20 miles in all, there is a fork in the road to Indian Park or the North Soda area. Take South Dry Fork Road here 8 more miles to a fence and a cattle guard at the entrance to Indian Park. Chances for seeing horses here are good. A return trip east down Winter Flats Road takes four-wheelers through more canyons and open range back to DeBeque. This road crosses numerous washes with big dips and ruts that appear after any rains.

•   Other access is possible via the *Mount Garfield Trail* near Palisade or the *Tellerico Trailhead* north of Grand Junction. Such routes are for experienced hikers and mountain horse riders, rather than first-time wild-horse watchers.

•   For more information on camping opportunities in the Little Bookcliffs, contact the Bureau of Land Management, 2815 H Road, Grand Junction, CO 81641; (970) 244-3000.

12
Marble, Colorado

Immense chunks of marble litter the landscape like toy building blocks left by a race of giants. White stones parallel a path like ruins of a prehistoric temple. Marble walls, two stories high, stand alone, connected to nothing. Large pieces of rusting machinery, cables, and decaying timbers are scattered everywhere. The scale of the rock pieces and the rusted machinery suggests that the work here was big and important. Indeed it was, but what you see in Marble is only the middle of the story. The beginning is in the massive mountain southeast of town; the end is in Washington D.C., Denver, and many other cities around the country.

Located in the Crystal River Valley, Marble's setting is Colorado mountain scenery at its best: aspen and spruce-fir forests, wildflowers, and waterfalls.

Within the dim reaches of geologic time, today's marble deposits of Treasure Mountain began as shells of organisms living in warm marine waters. When the animals died, they settled into layers and mixed with organic matter, including plants and other animals. Their calcite shells gradually cemented together to form limestone, and the organic matter caused it to take on a black coloration.

The geologic fate of this formation, laid down when dinosaurs were roaming a vast coastal plain, differs from location to location. Near Leadville, the limestone includes high concentrations of silver, lead, and zinc; this sort of limestone is called Leadville Limestone.

Near Marble, limestone was subjected to tremendous heat from volcanic activity. The upward flow of molten rock, called magma, caused a dome to form, and the magma pushed its way into the limestone layer causing the fine calcite grains to recrystalize, or metamorphose, into large crystals. Apparently the heat also cooked off the organic matter, leaving the rock a pure white, instead of black, like its limestone parent rock. There is only one other quarry in the world that has marble of such quality and translucence: Carrara, Italy.

A general store in Marble has elegant steps made from marble locally quarried. Information about the quarry may be obtained here and at other stores in town.

Crypto Scene

Marble was once the building material of choice for a growing nation that wanted to make a bold statement in its public buildings and monuments. Marble is durable, like granite, retains little moisture, and is fireproof. This white stone also makes a strong statement of permanence—just the right stuff for a nation. So where could the United States find the best building blocks available? Marble, Colorado.

Mill Around in Marble

Along the Crystal River are ruins of the Colorado-Yule Marble Company's finishing mill. The building, where rough-cut blocks from the quarry were cut and shaped into finished blocks, was more than 1,600 feet long, making it one of the largest stone finishing mills in the world. It is now part of a city park and visitors can see evidence of the milling operation.

There are megachunks of marble scattered along what was once the right-of-way for the Crystal River and San Juan Railroad that moved marble to cities across the nation. Tall stone pillars, partially hidden in trees on the north side of the right-of-way, were once part of the overhead crane system used to

The marble taken from Yule Creek today is quarried from deep within
the mountain. The scale of the modern quarry dwarfs humans and
machinery. At top, a shaft of sunlight highlights the lines of marble blocks
previously quarried.

move marble into the mill and shop areas. The pillars also supported the side walls of the shop.

Huge blocks of roughly cut marble were hauled down 3.5 miles from the stone quarry to the block yard and stored. The company experimented with several methods to transport the heavy blocks: mule power, steam tractors, and eventually electric tram railroads. Blocks were moved into the mill and cut into various shapes and sizes with diamond saws.

Columns for the Lincoln Memorial were made from large drums (slices of round, finished marble) that were fluted, and then shipped to Washington D.C., where they were then stacked one on top of the other. See if you can find a drum hidden in the undergrowth along the right-of-way. Could it have been a rejected piece of the Lincoln Memorial?

Look for the crumbling remains of a snow wall parallel to the Crystal River, on its north bank. In 1912, an avalanche destroyed the company office and Shop No.1. After several other avalanches roared down Mill Mountain, the company decided to build a wall of marble to protect the buildings. Only a portion of the wall remains today, but you can see that it was tilted to the south to deflect snow. The wall, constructed from waste marble blocks, was 15 feet thick and 65 feet high by 1916!

The quarry was originally located above Yule Creek on the face of the mountain, and as quarrying progressed, it moved inward and down the hill. Equipment and buildings clung precariously to the hillside. Marble quarried today comes from deep within the mountain. Because the work area is dangerous, the quarry is not always open to the public. Inquire at the general store to find out if the quarry is open.

The modern underground quarry is gargantuan. Very large front-end loaders seem tiny in the cavernous space of the quarry. Modern diamond-bladed chain saws are used to cut the blocks of marble from the face of the quarry walls; the stone is then skidded out and trucked down the mountain over a narrow road.

However hard the labor, quarry workers seem to love their jobs. Ferdinando Borghetti, an Italian quarryman, expressed his passion for the stone, telling sculptors that "this marble, she is from the heart." Sculptors who attend an annual marble symposium each July and August adopted his words as their motto—from the heart.

Back in Time Line

The discovery of these marble deposits was almost an accident. Prospectors entered the valley looking for silver. In 1884, a miner working his claim near Marble noticed "something peculiar" about the roof of his mine: "It is composed of as fine a marble as you will find anywhere." Not far away, and in the same year, the first marble quarry was opened on Rock Creek. As explorations of the area continued, an even larger deposit of marble was discovered along Yule Creek, and operations shifted to that area.

The columns of the Lincoln Memorial in Washington D.C. were milled from marble taken from the Yule Creek area. The geology curator from the U.S. Museum declared Yule marble "is not excelled by any marble in America."
National Park Service

Architectural fashions of the early 1900s created a demand for marble. In Denver, the Federal Courthouse, Cheeseman Park Memorial, and the Public Service Company Building at 15th and Champa Streets were constructed from Colorado-Yule marble. Utah, Indiana, Ohio, Oregon, New York, California, and Massachusetts all boast buildings made from the high-quality Colorado stone.

At Arlington National Cemetery, the Tomb of the Unknown Soldier is the greatest contribution that Colorado-Yule Marble has yet made to the nation. A special 56-ton block of marble was lovingly quarried and shipped to Vermont for finishing in 1931. The mammoth block of ornately carved marble now protects the remains of unknown soldiers who gave their lives to ensure the freedoms we enjoy today.

Colorado-Yule marble continues to be used for headstones in our national cemeteries and is regaining modest popularity in building construction. Long recognized for its translucent properties, this prized marble is fashioned into sculptures that grace art galleries and parks across the country and around the world.

- Marble is south of Glenwood Springs and Redstone, off Colorado 133, on Gunnison County 3.
- Camping is available at Bogan Flats, a U.S. Forest Service campground next to the Crystal River at Bogan Flats, about 2 miles toward Marble on Gunnison County 3, after you turn east off Colorado 133. Contact Gunnison National Forest, 2250 Highway 50, Delta, CO, 81416; (970) 874-7691, for more information. Accommodations are available in Marble and nearby Redstone.
- Crystal Mill is about 5 miles beyond Marble, on a four-wheel-drive road.

The remains of the marble wall constructed to protect the mill from avalanches is just to the left of the bridge timbers, on the north shore of the Crystal River.

13 Mesa Verde National Park

Prehistoric cities of stone have been standing silently within the sandstone alcoves of Mesa Verde for nearly 900 years. Intriguing, but eerie, the cliff dwellings leave many questions unanswered: Who lived here? Why did they leave? Where did they go? If you enjoy such mysteries, then Mesa Verde National Park is an ideal destination for you. Plan to be overwhelmed on your visit though. There are more than 4,000 known archaeological sites within Mesa Verde National Park, and many more in the surrounding area!

People who lived in cliff dwellings briefly flourished from 1100 to 1300 A.D. in the area we now call Mesa Verde, green table in Spanish. Until recently they were known as the Anasazi (ANA-sa-zi), ancient ones, or ancient enemies in the Navajo language, and to modern Pueblo Indians as Ancestral Puebloans. What these people called themselves is one of the many puzzles that may never be solved. For some modern-day visitors to the ruins, the ancient ones are still here, or at least the echoes of their voices. Listen carefully. Maybe they will speak to you. You may unlock secrets that many others have failed to find!

Climb into a Prehistoric World

Whoever lived here must not have feared heights. Find out how you would have liked cliff dwelling when you climb the ladders of Mesa Verde. Scary as it may seem, rising high onto cliff faces, crawling through tunnels, or entering dark underground ceremonial chambers was routine for this culture. As you retrace their steps, try to figure out how these ancient people entered their dwellings and conducted their daily chores. Put yourself in their place; think as they might have thought.

On the Road to Ruins

Mesa Verde National Park offers an amazing variety of ruins to visit. However, choosing which ones to see can be tough. There are two types of structures to see and explore: surface dwellings and cliff dwellings. The principal dwellings are found on either Chapin Mesa or Wetherill Mesa. Chapin Mesa is the most heavily visited area and provides more visitor services than Wetherill Mesa, including a museum and book store. Wetherill is less crowded and has more of a remote feeling.

A park ranger leads visitors up the 32-foot-high ladder into Balcony House. Climbing into the prehistoric dwellings is just the beginning of the adventure into the past.

Cliff Palace on Chapin Mesa housed nearly 250 people and must have been a very busy community at the height of its occupancy.

Many of the ruins require tickets to visit, so your first stop should be the Far View Visitor Center. In summer, arrive early to obtain guided-tour tickets in advance because tours fill rapidly. One of the most popular ruins is Balcony House on Chapin Mesa. The park service has installed a 32-foot-high ladder to enter Balcony House, where visitors explore the ruin by crawling through a narrow tunnel that the original inhabitants used. Warmed by the morning sun, east-facing Balcony House is a medium-size cliff dwelling with 40 rooms. Its unique features include a walled courtyard that was likely the center of activity for residents. The wall at the edge of the courtyard probably provided security for young children and a pleasant setting for food preparation or just visiting.

When exploring the ruins, ask yourself if these people were much different from us today. Their basic needs for food, shelter, safety, and hopes for the future were similar to those of people around the world today. Understanding how they met their needs bridges the past to help us know more about them. Look for links between our cultures and theirs. This will make these Ancestral Puebloans seem less like strangers while you investigate their homes.

Paleo Scene

If you happen to visit during a thundershower, you will understand how erosion that started millions of years ago created the canyon country that makes up the Mesa Verde of today. When the first people arrived here, this rugged country looked almost as it does now. Weather-resistant sandstone caps a softer layer of shale. The shale erodes rather quickly, but the hard sandstone protects it for a while, until big blocks of sandstone are undercut by wind and water, and eventually slump down the slopes.

We call the people who first settled here a prehistoric people, because they did not have a written language to record the events of their time. Like other early Native Americans, the Ancestral Puebloans traditionally passed information from one generation to another by telling stories, called an oral history. Because the Ancestral Puebloans did not have a written history and because there isn't a proven link to modern-day tribes, their stories have been lost. So their mysteries remain.

What we do know is that the area we now call Mesa Verde looks very similar to the way it appeared when the Ancestral Puebloans lived here. Seeds, fibers, and building materials found in the ruins are identical to types of plants found here today! By careful comparison of animal bones found in their trash heaps, archaeologists have determined that the same types of animals were here then as are now. The climate has changed very little here over the past 2,000 years; the area continues to receive less than 18 inches of rainfall a year.

Early inhabitants were dryland farmers who cultivated their crops on the mesa tops. Some evidence has been found of small check dams to trap water

The second-largest cliff dwelling, Long House, is on Wetherill Mesa. It was discovered in 1891 but was not excavated until 1959. Long House contains 21 kivas, or ceremonial chambers.

for modest garden plots. Archaeologists think they have also found evidence of irrigation ditches that moved water from one location to another.

By the late 1100s the people started to move into sandstone alcoves below the canyon rims and build homes of stone and mud mortar. Why did they move into the canyons below? The answer is unknown. There is little evidence that the cliff dwellings were built to escape raiders. Perhaps they liked living in small communities so that they could share the work of the pueblo. It may also have been simply that the rock overhangs afforded greater protection from the summer heat or the bitter winds of winter.

Crypto Scene

Mesa Verde is full of mysteries. What types of ceremonies were conducted in underground kivas? Why are there T-shaped doorways? What messages were these early inhabitants trying to communicate with their elaborate rock drawings?

Some of the consistent features you will find in the cliff dwellings and the surface pueblos on the mesa tops are sunken circular rooms. These rooms are ceremonial chambers, or kivas (KEE-vahs) in the Hopi language. Religious ceremonies held in these structures were probably an important part of the lives of these prehistoric people because they lived at the mercy of the elements. Too little rain, cold weather, scarce game, and sickness all contributed to their need to pray for the assistance of their spirit gods. At Long House Ruin there are 21 kivas. Can you imagine why Cliff Palace, the largest cliff dwelling with 80 rooms, has only seven kivas?

A kiva usually had a roof over it and entry was through a hole in the roof, which also let smoke from a fire pit escape. Archaeologists have found uniform features of kivas include a central fire pit, a stone deflector shield between a fresh-air ventilator shaft and the fire pit, a bench around the edge of the room, and stone columns, or pilasters, held up the roof.

The most important feature of a kiva is the sipapu (SEE-pah-pooh), or spirit hole, from which the Ancestral Puebloans may have believed their ances-tors entered the world from the underworld. They also may have believed that the sipapu enabled them to communicate with their ancestors. It's not known what other purposes the sipapu may have served.

Much speculation about these people is based on our knowledge of mod-ern pueblo people, such as the Hopi and other tribes found in the Southwest.The ceremonial kiva and the sipapu are still part of modern pueblo culture and provide some insights into daily patterns of the earlier culture.

Check out Spruce Tree House on Chapin Mesa where you can enter a restored kiva by descending a six-foot-long ladder into the dark, circular chamber. Because kivas are still important in religious practices of several modern-day pueblo people; enter with respect.

More Riddles Among the Ruins

As you explore Mesa Verde's other prehistoric ruins, be sure to look for

In refuse mounds below the cliff dwellings, numerous animal bones and plants, such as these corncobs, remain. This evidence reveals much about the daily life and diets of the ancient Pueblo people.

T-shaped doorways. Can you suggest why the builders would go to the trouble of creating such odd-shaped entries? There are no right or wrong answers to this question, because it may be impossible to know the answer. One explanations is that it made it easier for people to enter rooms when they were carrying heavy loads on their backs; they could stoop over and use the door ledge to help them enter. Another theory is that the upper, larger opening could be covered with an animal skin in the winter to reduce heat loss while allowing fresh air to enter through the bottom opening. Possibly, since the doorways are not found everywhere, the T shapes may have been a special style of construction for a particular clan or family.

Burials discovered by archaeologists also provide clues about these mysterious people. For example, their average height was less than that of people today. For women, the average height was about 5 feet. Men were slightly taller, at about 5 feet 4 inches or 5 feet 5 inches. They ground their corn with stone manos (MAH-no), or hand stones, that were rubbed back and forth on metates (MEH-tah-tay), or flat stones. Grit would become mixed with the corn and eaten along with it causing their teeth to wear down. Look for corn grinding tools when you visit some of the cliff dwellings. They lived, on average, only 32 to 34 years, probably because of the many hazards they faced, occasional food shortages, and harsh living conditions. More than half of the children born would not have lived beyond five years of age!

The yucca plant was a very useful source of materials in the daily lives of the Pueblo people. Its roots were pounded into soap, and its fibers were used as thread to lace mats together. The plant is still found at Mesa Verde.

Micro Scape

You may not think of the forest found around Mesa Verde as a grocery store, but the pueblo people found many of their daily needs met by plants found here. They relied on hunting game and harvesting the piñon nuts, prickly pear cactus, and other plants. The sinuous fibers of yuccas were used as thread to lace mat edges together, and the sharp points of the sturdy leaves were used as needles. Yucca roots were pounded into a soap, and the fruit was used as food.

Check out the juniper trees along the mesas. The inner bark was used for diapers because the stringy bark is absorbent and relatively soft! Juniper trunks and larger branches were frequently used as roof timbers, which help archaeologists date dwellings by using an accurate technique called dendrochronology, or tree-ring dating.

Archaeological investigations reveal that the people gradually began to cultivate crops of corn, beans, and squash, relying less on gathering wild plants. Their corn crops were not at all like the modern corn crops we see in Iowa or other Midwestern states. The corn stalks were very short, and individual ears of corn were only a couple of inches long!

You become more curious about what you may discover as you approach Mesa Verde. Your curiosity is similar to Richard Wetherill's, who was among the first white people to enter the cliff houses after hearing stories from Ute Indians.

In December 1880, Richard and his brother-in-law, Charlie Mason, discovered what are now called Cliff Palace, Spruce Tree House, and Square Tower House Ruins. Their family ranch was nearby, and it became a destination for tourists who wanted to visit the ruins.

The cliff dwellings are certainly the spectacular highlight of the prehistoric culture of Mesa Verde, but for 700 years before the prehistoric people began constructing their cliff houses, they lived in pit houses and pueblos on the mesa tops. The loop road to Square Tower Ruin leads you to some of these earliest pit houses.

From Pueblos to Palaces

There are several periods of occupation represented in the ruins found on Mesa Verde. Try to understand this occupation sequence.

Basket Maker is the name archaeologists have given to the first group of farming Indians who lived on the mesa tops. These enterprising individuals used the Mesa Verde area from the first century A.D. to 400 A.D. They were

Imagine the excitement of the Wetherill family, local ranchers, when they found the ancient cliff dwellings in the 1880s. This is John Wetherill, one of five Wetherill brothers. The Wetherills' initial discoveries led to full-scale scientific excavations that yielded important information about the early cultures of the Southwest, and added to the general body of knowledge about our past.

National Park Service

Small dioramas at the park museum on Chapin Mesa re-create Pueblo life within the cliff dwellings, providing a glimpse into the daily activities of the inhabitants. National Park Service

best known for making tightly woven baskets. They did not use bows and arrows. Very little has been learned about these people, and no occupation sites have been discovered within Mesa Verde National Park.

Around 500, a group of more advanced people called the Modified Basket Makers began to appear in Mesa Verde. It is unknown how their technology evolved or whether outside influences began to precipitate change. These people continued to make baskets, but a crude pottery type begins to appear in pit-house excavations. The pit-house dwellings were found not only on the mesa tops, but also within alcoves that would later contain the cliff pueblos.

Following the Modified Basket Maker culture, the Developmental Pueblo period began. About 750, these people started to build above-ground structures with several attached rooms. Communities began to develop and perhaps they began to share work and have a loose social structure. Their pottery-making improved, and the distinctive Mesa Verde black-on-white pottery was showing up more frequently as well as utilitarian corrugated pottery. These pottery types can be seen at the park museum. Research of these latest periods of development also revealed that the Ancestral Puebloans had elaborate trade routes that brought other pottery, turquoise, and seashell bracelets from the west coast!

The final and highest stage of development was the Great Pueblo Period (1100–1300) when masonry constructed multiroomed cliff houses were built, and a highly-evolved social structure had developed.

Gone for Good?

Suddenly the people vanished! By the early 1300s, the pueblos were abandoned and started to deteriorate. Tree-ring dating shows that a major drought occurred beginning in about 1276 and food became scarce. Maybe the numbers of people had become too great for their land and wildlife resources. This may be a lesson to us by the Ancestral Puebloans—that we are dependent on natural resources and that we must try to conserve their use, to save something for future generations.

Pueblos found on the Hopi mesas today, and the structures of many tribes in New Mexico, bear a remarkable resemblance to the prehistoric dwellings of the Ancestral Puebloans. Although evidence is not conclusive, many researchers believe these modern people are somehow related to the earlier people. The answer may never be known, but the mysteries that remain may be the legacy they have left us!

Travel Log

• Open year-round, Mesa Verde is in the southwest corner of Colorado, between Cortez and Durango on U.S. 160. The park has an excellent first-come, first-served campground, with 450 campsites. Obtain detailed information in advance to plan your trip, since many of the prehistoric dwelling tours require tickets and summer crowds cause early sellouts. Write Superintendent, Mesa Verde National Park, Mesa Verde, CO 81330. The Mesa Verde Museum Association has many fine publications, write PO Box 38, Mesa Verde, CO 81330; (800) 305-6053.

• Numerous motels and private campgrounds are available in adjacent communities.

At the Step House cliff dwelling on Wetherill Mesa archaeologists have created a cut-away of a pit house that allows visitors to see the method of construction and the interior of this early style house.

National Park Service

14
Pawnee National Grassland

Discovery Zone

Freedom is the feeling that strikes you at Pawnee National Grassland where the sky really is the limit. Approaching the grassland, rolling prairie stretches in all directions. From the Buttes Overlook, space sweeps to the horizon. In spring, a limitless blue sky tops off an ocean of green highlighted with yellows and pinks.

The expanse of Pawnee's picture-perfect shortgrass prairie has signs of life everywhere: Insects and rodents tunnel beneath the blue grama and buffalo grass, and shy antelope graze warily on the open range. There is always something interesting to enjoy at Pawnee.

Break Out the Binoculars!

Action happens miles before explorers reach the Briggsdale intersection on Colorado 14. Birds abound. Northern harriers hover, waiting to snatch unwary rodents from their grassy homes below. Ferruginous, red-tailed, and Swainson's hawks appear here and there, and burrowing owls cautiously peer out from prairie dog towns. An occasional coyote may even stalk by as herds of pronghorn speed away.

Once at the Crow Valley Recreation Area, you can stop and consider a picnic, biking, more bird-watching, or a pleasant drive to a hike along the white chalk cliffs of Pawnee Buttes. The Pawnee Self-Guided Birding Tour begins at this grove of elm and cottonwood trees, a favorite place for cookouts and camping. The 36-mile birding tour can be made by car or mountain bike on paved and gravel roads.

North of Crow Valley, the route to Pawnee Buttes takes adventurers away from modern conveniences into farming and ranching country. Along the way, lark buntings show off white wing patches as they dip and dive over pasture grasses. Stopping often to perch on fence posts, Colorado's state bird competes with meadowlarks for the attention of passersby. Beyond Grover, the tour turns into a broad, gravel road that passes by windmills, old and new. After 14 miles, a short spur takes visitors to a trailhead and overlook that offer panoramic prairie views.

West Pawnee Butte towers above acres of expansive prairie in eastern Colorado. A meandering trail to the butte guides hikers and bird watchers through a grassland ecosystem rich with plants and wildlife.

Hit the Trail!

• *Pawnee Buttes Trailhead*—Hikers take off from the Pawnee Buttes Trailhead and descend gentle slopes blanketed with thick grass, patches of prickly pear cactus, and clumps of yucca. Walking along the soft sandstone and clay trail, it is not hard to imagine the grassland as it must have been during the 1800s. Visions of bison roaming the plains easily give way to images of cowhands stringing barbed wire to fence their cattle in. Within a short distance, badlands bordered by cliffs on all sides appear. Here, above Lips Bluff, prairie falcons play in the wind, inviting hikers to continue for a view of the West Butte.

In 1.5 miles, you reach a 250-foot-high sandstone butte, with its twin off to the east. Short-horned lizards bask in the sun while horned larks bounce from rock to rock. Be cautious here: Eroding rocks can easily disintegrate and western rattlesnakes call this home. A stroll back to the trailhead can intrigue bird-watchers and botanists as kestrels dart along the cliffs and cushion plants dot the soft soil.

• The overlook and cliffs are closed to the public March 1 through June 30 to protect nesting birds of prey. If hikers approach nests, adult birds may desert their eggs or young birds. There is still an inspiring view from the trailhead, however, and the 1.5 mile hike has great vistas, too.

Curious but cautious, pronghorn can spring across the prairie at high speeds.

Paleo Scene

Just think, 80 million years ago, a trip to Pawnee would have required waders! An inland ocean covered what are rolling grasslands today. How do we know this ancient sea existed here? Evidence of the ocean bed remains in the shale soils of the badlands that break the sod of the prairie. Ripple marks in some rocks are actual impressions of the wave-lapped shore. Giant carnivorous fish may have lived in the sea, and four-ton dinosaurs that looked liked overgrown armadillos stomped on the sand! Later, mammals resembling camels and rhinoceroses appeared, only to become extinct as the climate changed. Much fossil evidence remains of these and other prehistoric animals throughout Pawnee National Grasslands, painting a vivid picture of the past.

After the sea started to retreat 65 million years ago, geologic uplifts occurred, draining the ocean and depositing layers of sediments. These deposits became the caprock that sits on top of the buttes. About 5 million years ago, more uplift occurred, and erosion washed away most of the soil. However, some of the hard sediments remained, protecting the underlying soft earth that was eventually carved into the present buttes. If this erosion had not happened, there would be no buttes at all!

You might stumble across 35-million-year-old fossils or Indian artifacts at Pawnee National Grasslands. If you find something, photograph it, and leave it in place for others to discover. Report special findings to the nearest federal or university archaeologist.

How do the cattle grazing on the grasslands find water to drink with so few streams around? That's what windmills are for! Throughout the prairie, antique and modern windmills lazily turn in gentle breezes or spin fiercely in stronger winds.

How does a windmill work? It harnesses wind power to pump water using wooden or metal blades that capture air currents. The spinning windmill turns a shaft that operates a pump that forces underground water up into a stock tank. The tank stays full, as long as occasional winds blow, which is most of the time on Colorado's plains. Modern windmills of various lightweight materials punctuate the Pawnee landscape, but a few wooden structures still whirl around on the wind-swept prairie to remind visitors of days gone by.

Wild Things

Every living thing in the grasslands is connected in one way or another. Black-tailed prairie dogs are a good example of this web of life. Living in large colonies, or towns, prairie dogs play host to an array of other wildlife, ranging from burrowing owls to hawks and foxes.

Prairie dogs survive by being alert to intruders such as golden eagles, coyotes, and people. Very social rodents, prairie dogs often sit on top of a mound of soil, clutching to family members in a group hug sort of way. Others stand as sentinels, to bark an alarm when predators are detected.

Get Along Little Doggies!

To escape such threats, prairie dogs have a complex system of underground tunnels and burrows where they live, sleep, and bear young. The sandy-furred little animals spend most of their time digging and repairing this network, packing dirt mounds around tunnel openings. Sleeping in their burrows at night, prairie dogs emerge early in the morning to feed on grasses and other plants. During the worst winter weather they stay underground, coming out only occasionally to feed.

In spring, prairie dogs give birth to litters of three to eight young, many of which fall victim to predators. Rattlesnakes not only eat young prairie dogs, they also move in and make the burrows their dens! Coyotes, foxes, and badgers eat prairie dogs, too, and they also prey on cottontail rabbits and deer mice that inhabit abandoned burrows.

Some of the most interesting sightings on the prairie are burrowing owls, which either take over abandoned prairie dog towns, or kick the prairie dog out of their own underground homes. Summer residents of Colorado's plains, these little owls hunt insects and mice, only occasionally preying on young prairie dogs. Spending much of their time on the ground, burrowing owls

Dark brown rivers of bison moved across the Colorado prairie in the mid-1800s. By 1884, most had been killed for their hides and meat. Some ranchers now raise bison for commercial purposes. Jim Flanigan

react to the warning barks of prairie dogs and scurry into their burrows when hawks or other predators approach.

Although prairie dogs are sometimes controversial because some ranchers believe that holes left by prairie dogs are hazards to stock, causing some cattle to break legs, biologists show that the animals are vital to the health of the prairie ecosystem. In addition to providing food for predators and shelter for other animals, prairie dogs are important cultivators. Their tunnels add air to the soil and they turn over fresh soil at burrow openings where an impressive variety of leafy plants may grow.

Micro Scape

What do prairie plants have in common with species living on alpine tundra? Drought, wind, sun, and rocky soil. In fact, many cushion plants growing on the exposed bases, sides, and caprock of Pawnee Buttes are the same type of plants that grow above 12,000 feet in elevation along Trail Ridge Road in Rocky Mountain National Park!

Blooming beautifully, as if in perfectly planned rock gardens, the delicate blossoms of sandwort and moss campion disguise their true hardiness. These low-growing mat and cushion plants, along with other prairie species have evolved to withstand blazing summer heat, hail storms, and winter winds that rake across the grasslands at 100 miles per hour. How do they survive? They grow close to the ground so that moisture-stealing winds blow right over them. They also have long water-seeking taproots that may make up as much as 90 percent of the entire plant.

Back in Time Line

Although there is some evidence of prehistoric Indians at Pawnee, more is known about the Plains Apache and Pawnee who left behind pottery before being forced out by Comanche and Ute Indians in the early 1700s. Arapaho, Cheyenne, and Sioux also spent time in the area to hunt bison that once numbered in the millions.

In the 1860s, railroads brought buffalo hunters to the area, and when settlers began to farm and ranch, Indians were forced out. By 1884, all the bison of the Pawnee Grasslands had been killed for their hides or to feed railroad construction crews, leaving nothing but room for cattle and crops. Over the years droughts chased many people away from the plains, but some hearty souls hung on to farm and ranch today. In 1960, the mix of private and public lands was designated the Pawnee National Grassland, now managed by the U.S. Forest Service.

Travel Log

• Pawnee National Grassland is 13 miles east of Ault, on Colorado 14. The best place to begin a bird-watching tour or an excursion to Pawnee Buttes is at the Crow Valley Recreation Area, 0.25 mile north of Highway 14 on Weld County (WCR) 77 near Briggsdale. From WCR 77, follow the Pawnee Pioneer Trails Scenic and Historic Byway northeast through Grover, 45 minutes to the Pawnee Buttes Trailhead.

• Spring is the most incredible season at Pawnee National Grassland, but summer and fall attract enthusiasts as well. Take along plenty of water, whether you plan to bike, hike, or just stroll around. For information write: District Ranger, Pawnee National Grassland, 660 O Street, Greeley, CO 80631; (970) 353-5004.

• Picnic, camping, and toilet facilities are available at the Crow Valley Recreation Area. Fees are charged for camping and for use of the Steward J. Adams Education Site, a special facility for outdoor education groups.

• *Pawnee Pioneer Trails Scenic and Historic Byway* — A 125-mile, 2-hour trip, begins in Ault, jogs north at Briggsdale, and loops through Grover, south to Raymer, and ends either in Sterling or Fort Morgan.

15
Picket Wire Canyonlands

Discovery Zone

It sounds like distant thunder echoing back and forth across the valley and rolling off the surrounding hills. You imagine the rumble to be the footsteps of enormous animals. Are there dinosaurs nearby? Then you look around this shortgrass prairie and realize, to your relief, that the rumble you heard was indeed thunder— not a herd of apatosaurs.

At Picket Wire Canyon south of La Junta you can arrange for a guided trip into the past. You need a four-wheel-drive vehicle to enter this rugged terrain, or you can hike the narrow and steep road into the core of the canyonlands, mountain bike, or ride in by horseback. If you go on foot, be sure to wear sturdy hiking shoes and carry an adequate supply of water to guarantee that you make it all the way to the one of the most awesome dino destinations in the state!

Paleo Scene

Along a stretch of the Purgatoire River bed, are footprints from more than 150 million years ago. At this remote site, curious adventurers can investigate the longest documented dinosaur trackway in North America! Extending more than 700 feet, these distinct tracks were left by a family of Jurassic-age dinosaurs in the sands of a shallow lake, now exposed in the sandstone of the old lakeshore.

Picket Wire Canyon has more than 1,300 dinosaur footprints that record the passage of individual dinosaurs as well as evidence of herd behavior. Scientists have identified more than 100 trackways on four levels of a prehistoric mudflat. After detailed analysis, they have determined that for every six meat-eating theropod tracks, there are 40 plant-eating sauropods, a ratio of plant-eating animals to meat-eaters that approaches the same proportions found in large wild animal populations today: approximately 1 to 30.

Dinosaur footprints along the Purgatoire River in southeast Colorado stir our imagination and our curiosity. For 150 million years these fossil prints have frozen the past for others to see. U.S. Forest Service

Do You Know Your Dinosaurs?

Paleontologists believe that the prehistoric landscape of Picket Wire may have appeared very much like today's African savanna—fairly flat, with occasional lakes and rivers—and enough vegetation to sustain dinosaur populations. At least two major types of tracks have been found. The first set is a group of quadruped, or four-footed, dinosaurs, probably sauropods, lizard-footed, animals. Five sauropods called apatosaurs, also known by their earlier name as brontosaurs, were traveling together along the edge of the water as they moved north, perhaps in search of food. The second group of tracks were bipedal, two-footed dinosaurs, meat-eating theropods. These tracks may have been made by a three-toed allosaur whose distinct trails are found right beside the apatosaur tracks. Were they lurking behind the gentle plant-eating giants looking for an easy meal?

Accurate interpretation of dinosaur tracks is challenging. Matching tracks to specific dinosaurs is almost impossible since there were so many closely related dinosaurs. For example, there is no certainty that a specific track belongs to a particular set of fossil foot bones, even if they were found nearby. Scientists make some guesses, but it is generally safer to say that tracks are brontopodus (track of a brontosaur), which suggests that the tracks belong to a certain scientific family of dinosaurs without specifying which particular member of the family.

Paleontologist Martin Lockley has been studying these trackways for years and calls the trackways found in Picket Wire Canyon "the most extensive set of dinosaur trackways in North America." If you want to become a paleontologist, he recommends that you "study biology and geology, and get a lot of experience observing the natural world." A student should "learn to be a good observer of animal behavior, and learn to identify rocks, minerals, fossils, and living fauna and flora." Martin's father was a naturalist and Martin was raised on a farm where he developed a strong curiosity about the natural world. In college, he became intested in paleontology because of an inspiring teacher.

Crypto Scene

Have you ever experienced the excitement of finding a fossil? Did you know that you had discovered an important sign of prehistoric life? People often think of fossils only as ancient bones that have turned to rock. But fossils can also be impressions of rain drops from storms millions of years ago, or dinosaur eggs, or a butterfly such as those at Florissant, or even animal droppings, or scat. The important thing to remember is that all this evidence contributes to our understanding of the prehistoric world.

The tracks of a theropod, filled with rainwater, are found next to the tracks of its source of food—a four-footed sauropod. Following their footsteps gives one an eerie feeling of walking into a prehistoric setting. U.S. Forest Service

Making Good Impressions

There are two theories about how fossil tracks or other impressions are preserved. The oldest idea is the cover-up theory: The creation of an imprint of a passing animal, or plant leaf, seed, or even an insect begins when the print is made in a relatively soft and moist substrate, like sand or mud. The print then dries and hardens in the sun, reducing the possibility of destruction. Next, a gradual deposit of softer material fills in and covers up the depression. Once buried, it's protected. After the overlying softer material is eroded away, it leaves the harder rock impression of the fossil plant or animal. At Picket Wire tracks occasionally disappear, and the softer material must be removed to reveal the trail's continuation.

The second theory of track preservation is that the weight of passing dinosaurs created impressions under the surface of the land as well. This made a hidden or "ghost" track. Already covered up, the footprints were much more likely to survive. So, while the surface footprint may have been erased by a flood or other disturbance, the underlying ghost track was protected.

Footnotes to History

Like a detective's findings at a crime scene, your observations can reveal clues about the prehistoric environment of the dinosaurs. When you visit the track site, be prepared to ask some questions. Did the dinosaurs pass this way at the same time? Are there more than two types of dinosaurs here? How wet was this substrate when a dinosaur family passed this way?

Carefully examine the tracks of each of the five apatosaurs. Do they occur at the same depth? Are they about the same size? A consistency in the size and depth of the tracks suggest that the animals were about the same size. It also implies that the consistency and moisture of the surface were the same, so all the animals made the tracks at once. Parallel tracks of different depths and sizes suggest that impressions were made at different times, perhaps weeks or months apart.

Trying to unravel the mystery of social behavior of prehistoric animals involves a lot of speculation and comparison with modern animals. A major question among scientists is whether the sauropods showed any herd instincts. Sauropod tracks at Picket Wire Canyon are generally evenly spaced. This intertrackway spacing is similar to that of large animals today that seem to maintain a constant distance between individuals. Follow the dinosaur trackway for a couple of hundred feet. Do the parallel tracks all turn at the same time? Can you guess if dinosaurs were avoiding some obstacle? Were they walking around an inlet to avoid a muddy spot? Signs of such uniform behavior could prove that some dinosaurs may have passed here at the same time.

Micro Scape

Occasionally the fossil record supplies details that you might think are impossible to detect after 150 million years. Some of these amazing finds occur along the impressive trackway at Picket Wire Canyon. You may find evidence of plant stems and freshwater clams trampled by a large sauropod. You may also see the skin pattern on the soles of dinosaur feet! You can even look for claw marks in the mud and tiny fossil droplets of water caused when the heavy animals splashed in the water.

Distance between track is an important detail. Find two tracks from the same foot of one dinosaur. Measure the space between them and repeat the process along the trackway. Do they stay the same distance apart or increase in distance? This information may tell you if the animal was maintaining a constant pace. The speed of dinosaurs has been estimated at 2 to 4 miles an hour for large sauropods and 4 to 6 miles an hour for large theropods. Who do you think would win in a race: the plant-eater, or the meat-eater?

Back in Time Line

Taking a trip to Picket Wire Canyonlands is like walking into an encyclopedia of local history. Within a short stretch of the Purgatoire River Valley are signs of life from 150 million years ago to as recent as the last century. Paleontological, archaeological, and historical clues are scattered across the landscape like Easter eggs!

There's More Than Dinosaurs

The name of the river is a bit of a mystery. Spanish soldiers and explorers seeking treasures died in the valley, and because they did not have a religious burial, their souls were condemned to be in a state of temporary suffering until they could be admitted to heaven. As a result, the river was called El Rio de Las Animas Perdidas en Purgatorio, or the River of Lost Souls in Purgatory. French explorers, upon hearing this legend, named the river the Purgatoire which Americans pronounced Picket Wire.

Signs of human passage through the curving canyons carved by the Purgatoire are usually obvious, but sometimes not. Search carefully for rock art sites. Some petroglyphs, or rock pictures, are etched into stone right along the trail! Pictographs, pictures painted on the rocks, are also found in the area, often side by side with carved images.

These symbols represent animals, humans, and geometric patterns. Determining what they mean and how old they are have challenged archaeologists for many years. There have been many theories developed about the significance of such symbols. Prehistoric people assigned spiritual meaning to much of the world around them, so etching the symbol of their favorite game species may have represented a religious effort to replenish dwindling numbers of animals or to ensure hunting success.

As you hike or drive into Picket Wire Canyon, you will see evidence of more recent human occupation. A cemetery and the remains of the Dolores Mission mark efforts of Mexican settlers to establish a community in the valley between 1871 and 1889. Reading the dates on the tombstones of these hardy

Petroglyphs—prehistoric evidence of another kind—are images carved into the rocks within the last several hundred years and are found along the trail.

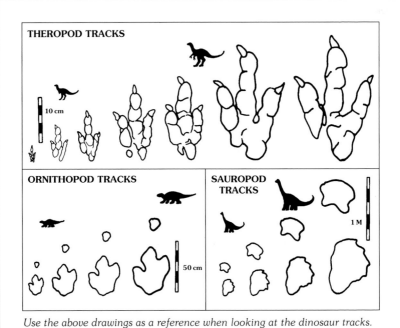

Use the above drawings as a reference when looking at the dinosaur tracks. Because not every print is perfect, it may be necessary to examine several tracks to confirm the type of dinosaur you are tracking.

people makes you wonder how tough life must have been for them. Be careful when exploring the mission ruins and cemetery because the old adobe walls are crumbling and rattlesnakes hide in the vegetation and under debris.

Cattle ranching empires used Picket Wire Canyonlands, too, and left behind corrals and occasional small buildings. One ranch, the Wineglass or Rourke Ranch, established in 1871, operated for 100 years. You can see the main ranch buildings about 3.5 miles beyond the dinosaur trackway.

A schoolgirl from Higbee told her science teacher about tracks that her father and a friend had found in 1935, and this led to scientists coming to study the trackway. Keep good notes, make sketches and maps, and take photographs as you explore remote areas in Colorado. Your observations may be important to the future of paleontology!

•   When investigating rock-art sites, the cemetery and mission ruins, and the ranches in Picket Wire Canyon, be respectful of these important features and remains of earlier human activity. Take only photos and leave only footprints.

• The dinosaur tracks can be seen on your own by hiking, mountain biking, or horseback riding along a wide dirt track, a 10.5-mile round-trip.The U.S. Forest Service offers guided tours, but you must have a four-wheel-drive vehicle to negotiate the rugged descent from Withers Canyon to the dinosaur track site. Reservations must be made well in advance. Contact Comanche National Grassland, 1420 E. 3rd St., La Junta, CO 81050; (719) 384-2181.

Visiting Picket Wire Canyonlands on Your Own

• Drive east from Pueblo on U.S. 50 to La Junta. From La Junta, take Colorado 109 south for 13 miles and head west on Otero County 802 for 8 miles. Proceed south (left) on County Road 25 for 6 miles. Turn left (east) on Forest Service Road 500A for 0.75 mile and go through the wire gate. Proceed another 2.0 miles until the road forks; take the left fork to a parking area and a pipe gate. The road is generally passable, but if your vehicle has minimal ground clearance, you can park at the beginning of Forest Service Road 500A and begin your journey at this point.The distance from the pipe gate to the dinosaur tracks is 5.3 miles one way. Start your trip early in the day; overnight camping is not permitted.

• You must be in good physical condition for this excursion. There is a 500-foot elevation difference from where you park your vehicle and the trackway. There is no drinkable water, so bring at least one gallon of water per person. If you visit the area in summer, temperatures range from 90° to 105° F. and afternoon thunderstorms may occur. For additional safety tips, current conditions, and detailed planning information write or call the national forest office.

Four-Wheel-Drive Guided Trips

• The reservation dates for guided trips to the dinosaur trackway are limited. You must make reservations well in advance of your visit. There is a small fee. Note that adverse weather may cause the trip to be canceled. Watch the weather forecast and keep in touch with the Comanche National Grassland staff, especially if you are making a long trip to La Junta.

16
Rocky Mountain Arsenal

Everybody gets a bird's-eye view from the top of the bright red double-decker tour bus at the Rocky Mountain Arsenal National Wildlife Refuge near Denver. Riding high above the shortgrass prairie, wildlife-watchers can spot a hawk or spy a deer from some of the best seats in the state! The refuge bus tour takes visitors past blue fishing lakes, signs of old homesteads, remnants of military history, and through one of the richest wildlife habitats in Colorado.

It is hard to imagine all this wildlife thriving amid a government Superfund site, an area of intense environmental cleanup. It was less than sixty years ago that the U.S. Army began to make weapons here during World War II.

A double-decker bus takes wildlife-watchers to Rattlesnake Hill where tour guides tell the human side of the arsenal story. Now a national wildlife refuge, the arsenal was originally set aside for military weapons production.

Refuge lakes invite anglers of all ages to test their skills during the annual fishing season between mid-April and mid-October. Because fishing arsenal waters requires catch-and-release practices, refuge fish sometime grow to great size and live long lives. Battling such experienced fish provides enjoyable challenges to anglers. Even if none are caught, arsenal lakes are a peaceful place to spend the day within a close drive of Denver.

Aboard the bus, tour-takers settle down with binoculars and field guides, ready to view some of the 300 animal species that live on the refuge. Depending on the season, you may see prairie dog pups emerge from burrows, bald eagles roost in cottonwoods, and bright orange orioles, or Swainson's hawks. Mule and white-tailed deer are a year-round highlight of the 27-square-mile reserve.

Everyone participates in spotting wildlife, letting others know where to look. Sometimes, lucky first-time bird-watchers notice white pelicans on Lake Ladora, prompting oohs and aahs from fellow observers. Excitement mounts with every bend in the road.

"Great blue heron to the right!"

"Red-tailed hawk up ahead!"

Everyone leaves a satisfied wildlife-watcher.

This is No Fish Story

Arsenal anglers don't need to tell fish stories. Many fish in Lake Mary, Lake Ladora, and Lower Derby Lake are the kind of whoppers heard about in fish tales. Trophy fish, like a 20-pound, 43-inch-long northern pike hauled out of Lake Ladora, are the result of more than a dozen years of catch-and-release fishing.

Lake Mary is a great place to introduce young anglers to the sport. A floating boardwalk leads past cattails and over water that is home to bluegill, bullfrogs, muskrats, toads, and salamanders. Those who have a Colorado fishing license and a special permit (issued each year by lottery) can stake out a favorite spot and try their luck. Whenever a fish is caught, it must be immediately unhooked and returned to the water unharmed.

The biological health of arsenal waters is monitored regularly by the U.S. Fish and Wildlife Service, and long-term studies are being conducted to maintain a healthy fish population.

All anglers must follow special fishing regulations published by the Rocky Mountain Arsenal National Wildlife Refuge; those under 16 years of age do not need a Colorado fishing license.

Wild Things

Bald eagles are one of the main reasons that Rocky Mountain Arsenal became a national wildlife refuge. In 1986, a winter communal roost, a gathering and resting area of bald eagles, an endangered species, was discovered along First Creek. The eagles were attracted to a cottonwood grove where they found food, shelter, and protection from human disturbance. The U.S. Fish and Wildlife Service became involved in managing the eagles and other wildlife at the arsenal during the environmental cleanup in 1987,

Refuge mule deer thrive on the doorstep of metropolitan Denver. An amazing variety of more than 330 species of mammals, reptiles, birds, fish, and amphibians live at the Rocky Mountain Arsenal.

and public interest led to the establishment of Rocky Mountain Arsenal National Wildlife Refuge in 1992.

In winter, visitors may see as many as 50 eagles along First Creek from the Eagle Watch viewing site that is equipped with spotting scopes and closed-circuit televisions.

Eagles are not the only raptors, or birds of prey, though. Swainson's hawks, red-tailed hawks, ferruginous hawks, great horned owls, and burrowing owls also share the refuge. Why? Because some of the best meals around can be found at the arsenal!

Even though the refuge is surrounded by Denver, Montbello, and Commerce City, its woodlands, wetlands, and grasslands offer great habitat for mice, ground squirrels, pocket gophers, and prairie dogs. Many raptors and other migratory birds stop at the refuge in spring after spending the winter in Central and South America. Here they nest, raise their young, and enjoy the abundant prey.

Unlike prairie dogs and other prey, deer at the refuge have few worries. Although coyotes occasionally hunt young or sick animals, mule and white-tailed deer are seen everywhere. White-tailed deer display the bright, white underside of their tails like a flag; this eastern species stays closer to the arsenal's woodlands than do bolder mule deer that are characterized by large ears, branching antlers, and black-tipped tail.

There may be too many deer though, because a fence surrounds the refuge and no hunting is allowed. Deer compete more for forage on the refuge and generally live longer than other Colorado deer. As more fawns increase the herd size, biologists work to manage the refuge deer population to keep vegetation available for all wildlife.

Back in Time Line

When settlers arrived in the mid-1800s, they displaced bison and American Indians with cattle and homesteads.

Changing Times on the Prairie

The settlers worked hard to maintain crops and homes on lands that were once windswept prairie. They planted windbreaks of cottonwood trees and dug irrigation canals to ensure water supplies. Sometimes nature challenged them with hailstorms, grasshoppers, and dust storms. In 1942, during World War II, the United States War Board announced that 19,833 acres of farmland and prairie would become the site of Rocky Mountain Arsenal. About 200 families had to leave their farms. Gunnar Herskind recalls, "We all remembered Pearl Harbor. When Uncle Sam needed our land, we were willing to help in any way we could."

By the end of the war, the arsenal had produced more than 100,000 tons of munitions; it remained an active military post into the 1980s. The munitions plants were converted to production of agricultural chemicals and pesticides, and private companies leased some of the buildings for manufacturing. These operations kept arsenal facilities operating in case of another national emergency.

The manufacture of chemical weapons and pesticides left wastes that affected water and wildlife. Some cleanup began in the 1950s, when contaminated liquids were drained into natural basins, but concern about groundwater quality and the health of waterfowl put a stop to this water pollution in the 1970s. Dedicated reclamation began in 1987 after the area was designated a government Superfund site. Cleanup will take years.

Crypto Scene

The National Eagle Repository, located in an inconspicuous building on arsenal land, plays an unusual role in the protection of bald eagles and other endangered or threatened raptors. For centuries, eagle feathers have been used by Indians in religious ceremonies. Bald and golden eagles were killed and parts used in healing, marriage, and naming ceremonies. By 1940, it became necessary to protect bald eagles, and later golden eagles, due to habitat loss, pesticides, and poaching. Strict laws now prohibit killing eagles.

A collection point for dead bald and golden eagles, the National Eagle Repository provides American Indians with feathers for cultural purposes. U.S. Fish and Wildlife Service personnel explain the process to special tour groups.
U.S. Fish and Wildlife Service

In the early 1970s, the U.S. Fish and Wildlife Service established the National Eagle Repository to provide a way for American Indians to obtain eagles and their feathers, talons, and wings for religious and cultural purposes. This helps to protect the birds.

Unfortunately, some birds still fall victim to hunters or in accidents with cars or power lines. People who find such birds can report to federal or state wildlife personnel, and the birds can be sent to the National Eagle Repository where they are preserved by freezing. Each eagle is assigned a number and tracked through a database. There is such a demand that birds are only kept from three to five days before being shipped out. About 3,000 people apply for an eagle each year, and more than 800 eagles are made available, thus discouraging illegal hunting and helping to maintain Indian rights and traditions.

Travel Log

- Take Interstate 25 to Interstate 70 north and east of Denver. Travel east on Interstate 70 to Quebec Street and head north along the west boundary of the refuge. There is a large parking lot at the West Gate at 72nd Avenue and Quebec. The arsenal is open only on Saturdays, and a free shuttle takes visitors to the main area.
- To make reservations for bus tours, winter eagle watching at the Eagle Watch Site, site tours, or to obtain more information, contact the U.S. Fish and Wildlife Service at (303) 289-0232.
- Refuge fishing permits are required. Contact Rocky Mountain Arsenal National Wildlife Refuge, Building 613, Commerce City, CO 80022-1748; (303) 289-0232 ext. 130.

Visitor Safety

Visitor safety is very important at the Rocky Mountain Arsenal National Wildlife Refuge. Because environmental cleanup is underway, public access is carefully controlled. All special programs require reservations and are guided by trained staff and volunteers. For further information on the cleanup, contact the U.S. Army at (303) 289-0136 or the Environmental Protection Agency at (303) 294-1130.

17

Rocky Mountain National Park

Discovery Zone

Rocky Mountain National Park will make a naturalist out of you. Once you see a soaring golden eagle or climb up a granite peak, you'll be hooked. You will notice sights and sounds in a different way, everywhere you go—even in your own backyard!

Sweet-smelling ponderosa pines in the low montane forests are an appetizer to miles of cool subalpine forests that lead to alpine tundra. Life here is wild and natural—something to savor.

Tools of the Naturalist's Trade

Most park visitors already have tools to capture the full flavor of the park's ecosystems. For some, their senses are enough. For others, a camera or binoculars may be essential. Combine either approach with careful observation and keen interest, and anyone can become a great naturalist in Rocky Mountain National Park!

• Watch out for wildlife! More birds, mammals, fish, amphibians, and insects live here than you can count. Understanding animal behavior is the only way to guarantee a successful wildlife watching experience. Read about the seasonal habits of raptors, elk, bighorn sheep, mule deer, and other animals as you prepare for your trip to the national park. Keep a guidebook and binoculars ready when you arrive so that you can easily view animals from your vehicle. Remember to watch all animals from a distance, even small rodents such as ground squirrels and chipmunks. If you approach too closely, either you or the animal may get hurt. Keep notes to track your wildlife observations from year to year. A wildlife checklist can be used at home, too!

• Picture this! For more than a century, artists have played an important role in preservation by using art and photographs to promote national parks. By the time the park was established in 1915, almost 40 other national parks and monuments had been set aside with the support of painters such as Albert Bierstadt and photographers like William Henry Jackson. Today, anyone with a camera, a sketch pad, a pencil, or some paints, can experience the same inspiration such artists felt among the Rocky Mountains. Find a quiet moment in a campground or take a break on a long hike. Focus on a subject, large or

The broad, flower-dotted meadows of Moraine Park typify the lower montane ecosystem of Rocky Mountain National Park. Four distinct layers of life are visible from the verdant banks of the Big Thompson River: the riparian, montane, subalpine, and alpine ecosystems. National Park Service

small, and capture your vision on film or paper. Use your images as a record of your observations in the national park.

• Step into science! Researchers study the park's air, water, climate, geology, and ecosystems. Scientists have discovered that low, bushy krummholz (German for crooked wood) at treeline holds clues about worldwide weather patterns. Adapted to survive freezing temperatures, changes in these twisty trees could point out global warming shifts. When you visit the tundra, imagine how changes in climate might affect treeline.

Paleo Scene

It is plain to see why this place is called rocky. Evidence of geologic action surrounds you. Geologic forces shaped this landscape slowly, the way a sculptor carves a choice piece of stone. Almost 2 billion years ago, shifting continental plates wedged, faulted, and contorted the earth here into

Persistent glaciers slowly sculpted U-shaped valleys from steep canyons throughout the park. Above Bear Lake, ice age scraping and plucking remains evident between Hallett Peak and Flattop Mountain where Tyndall Glacier sits today. National Park Service illustration by Robert W. Tope

metamorphic rocks called gneiss, schist, marble, and quartz. Then volcanic materials squeezed up into cracks, forming bands of granite and pegmatite.

Many millions of years later, more molten lava surfaced, forming the pinkish rock of Longs Peak and Lumpy Ridge. After several periods of erosion and sinking beneath ancient seas, the Rocky Mountain region was gradually pushed upward again, forming massive blocks of stone that were later smoothed and shaped by wind and weather.

About 25 million years ago, volcanoes made a repeat performance, and for the next 2 million years, smoke billowed over the landscape, depositing fine-grained ash hundreds of feet deep, welded by heat into rock. Two examples of this fiery time can be observed along Trail Ridge Road at Lava Cliffs and Specimen Mountain. When the last phase of uplifting occurred about 21 million years ago, the smoothly eroded surfaces of the mountains rose to their final heights, tipping stream drainages and producing steep V-shaped canyons.

More recently, snow accumulated in the heads of the canyons. As temperatures cooled, snow compressed into layers so deep that summer sun could not melt them. Masses of ice resulted, many miles long, and hundreds of feet thick, filling every major valley with solid, slow-moving frozen rivers. These fingers of ice clawed at the steep canyon walls, plucking away at their sides and grinding the granite into wide U-shaped valleys. Glacial cirques, or bowls, were scooped out just below the highest peaks.

You can see Ice Age history throughout the park. Bear Lake offers a particularly impressive view of ancient sculpture. Tyndall Glacier, in the U-shaped valley between Hallett Peak and Flattop Mountain, remains as one of five still-active glaciers in the park.

Wild Things

Rocky Mountain National Park is packed with wildlife: While mule deer, chipmunks, marmots, and coyotes thrive, other animals struggle to survive. What affects the success of wildlife? Some species battle natural elements while others are more influenced by human activities such as traffic, development, and pollution.

Symbol of Rocky Mountain

As many as 4,000 bighorn sheep lived in this area until the mid-1800s, then herds were devastated by hunting, habitat loss, and disease. By 1915, bighorn had declined to about 1,000 sheep. Records show that after reaching a low of only 190 individuals in 1935, bighorn herds began a slow recovery. Thanks to protection, bighorn sheep now number about 600.

Both male and females have horns, but only the males use them for defense and to fight for mating rights. Rams, that can weigh as much as 400

Bighorn sheep thrill alert wildlife watchers. During mating season, rams duel for power by striking blows with their massive horns. A bighorn with a full curl may have endured up to 20 years of such challenges. Jim Flanigan

Stately bull elk fill the crisp autumn air with haunting mating sounds or bugles. Each fall, males use their imposing antlers in battles with competing bulls to establish dominance over a group of cow elks. Jim Flanigan

pounds, rely on their muscular necks to serve as shock absorbers during heavy-duty head-butting sessions each winter. Notice that a ram's horns curl and are ringed with annual growth marks that help determine its age. A three-quarter curl indicates an age of about 10 years. Mature bighorn can live up to 15 or 20 years in the wild.

The greatest threat to bighorn is human-caused stress. They can become confused around cars and people, and such tension makes them susceptible to diseases. At Bighorn Mountain, where sheep descend to visit the natural mineral licks at Sheep Lakes, a seasonal Bighorn Crossing sign allows the animals to safely traverse U.S. 34.

Leaders of the Band

Who are the most musical members of Rocky Mountain National Park's wildlife band? Without a doubt—bugling bull elk. The unearthly call of a 750-pound bull elk can send shivers down your spine. In fall, during the breeding season, or rut, elk gather in meadows where males compete for the attention of females, cows. This time of year is tough on the animals because of the competition to mate. Bulls spar with other bulls to impress cows and to display their enormous, branching antlers, that can weigh as much as 25 pounds and spread as wide as 4.5 feet. The bulls prod, poke, and puncture the competition—sometimes fatally.

An elk's antlers break off bit by bit and are finally shed. In spring, new antlers bud and grow, nourished by a covering of blood-rich velvet. When the rack is full-grown, its velvety skin sheds as elk rub their antlers against tree trunks.

Elk migrate to the lowlands when snows blanket higher elevations. Seeking shelter in forests by day, elk are most often seen grazing in meadows at dawn or dusk. Elk gnaw aspen bark when food is scarce in winter. You might notice that the scars are high above the ground. Picture an aspen forest when the ground is covered with 6 feet of snow—and an elk standing on top of that frozen platform—you will understand how those marks seem to be out of reach!

Natural Born Builders

While rain, wind, and snow continue to shape the park, a smaller force, beaver, also rearrange the landscape—sometimes overnight! One afternoon you may see a trickling stream, and the next morning, a pond has formed behind a well-built dam of sticks and mud.

Hidden Valley Creek, the Big Thompson River, and the Colorado River show evidence of beaver activity. In some places, beaver continually alter the course of these waterways, creating a changing environment for animals such as greenback cutthroat trout, mallard ducks, and seldom-seen river otters. Where you notice pointed stumps of aspen trees, wood shavings scattered on the ground, or a trail of flattened grass near a pond or stream, your chances of seeing beaver are better than good.

Beaver lodges may appear to be great piles of sticks and mud, but they are actually well-designed homes for entire families of these skilled builders. A lodge features one large room that can be reached by underwater passages. Two adults, three to four yearlings, and three to four kits — or newborns — dwell in the cone-shaped structure. When the pond freezes in winter, beaver swim under the ice to collect food.

National Park Service illustration by Bill Border

Adult beaver grow to a length of 3 feet (including their tail) and can weigh 50 pounds. Super swimmers, beaver zip around in water, but they are less impressive on land. To escape predators such as coyotes, bobcats, or mountain lions, they head back to water where they can create a surprising warning with the slap of a flat tail.

When beaver move into a wetland, they build dams. They gnaw aspen, willow, and alder and float freshly cut branches to the construction site through canals. Then they push the green limbs into the streambed to make a foundation and add layers of mud and sticks to complete the dam. Ponds above dams provide habitat for other wildlife. When silt eventually fills the ponds and dams break, meadows form. The beaver may move on or start their work all over again. To compare what changes beaver produce in the landscape, draw a sketch or take a photo of a place with signs of beaver. Bring this reference on your next visit to the park. You may be in for quite a surprise!

Crypto Scene

On a moonlit summer night near treeline, krummholz seem to march by ridgeline rocks like spirits in a ghostly procession. Embers glow deep within a pit, sparks fly from the fire. Quick scraping sounds break the stillness as hunters bend low, sharpening their projectile points for the next kill.

Adventurous hikers negotiate a narrow ledge on 14,255-foot, square-topped Longs Peak. The highest peak in the park was named for Major Stephen H. Long, leader of a U.S. Army survey expedition across the Great Plains in 1820.

It takes a real detective to examine the landscape of Rocky Mountain National Park and come up with clues to write a story like this. Parts of the puzzle may rest buried beneath 6 feet of soil or scattered along the frozen ground. Yet research and patience helps scientists to conjure up this image of a setting somewhere along Trail Ridge Road—almost ten thousand years ago.

Human activity occurred in this area long before the Ute and Arapaho made their summer home here. Try to detect the barely visible traces of early human history in the park: a row of rocks, low walls, cairns, and depressions in the soil. Archaeologists recognize these as snapshots of a prehistoric life when wolves, grizzly bears, and even bison were on these rocky ridges.

Some of the high uplands in the park still have ancient game-drives used by prehistoric hunters. These resourceful people built rock walls along certain well-traveled routes used by deer and elk. The fences funneled animals downwind toward hunters who were hidden by large boulders or man-made rock blinds. The hunters ambushed the game animals and then butchered them, using stone knives and scrapers.

Archaeologists use radiocarbon dating to determine the age of charcoal grains from ancient campfire sites. They can analyze the growth of lichens on rocks within the game-drive structures, and knowledge about the weathering rate of granite also helps to determine dates. Research indicates that distinct hunting events occurred in the park from 220 to 9,390 years ago (not long after the last ice age ended!)

Micro Scape

Like an endless green lawn, alpine tundra covers one-third of Rocky Mountain National Park and is inviting when temperatures soar in valleys below. Summer is short on the tundra, and organisms must be tough to grow and survive in this land of no trees.

Bright orange in fall and white in winter, the tundra resembles places in Alaska or Canada where extreme climates determine how plants live. Just how fierce are tundra conditions? Above 11,200 feet in elevation, winds howl at speeds of more than 100 miles per hour. Temperatures remain below freezing for at least five months each year and more than 40 feet of snow falls annually. Even with so much snow, tundra soils stay dry because winter winds sweep most of the moisture away. One final challenge cannot be overlooked—twice as much ultraviolet light bombards tundra plants through this thin atmosphere. How in the world do tiny tundra plants battle such terrible odds? Most have adapted to their severe surroundings.

Some plants such as phlox and moss campion grow round and squat, like pincushions, so that winds pass right over them. Their leaves trap bits of flying dirt that stack up into valuable soil. Another alpine survivor, mountain candytuft produces a white, waxy layer of cells that keep moisture from escaping. Sweet-smelling forget-me-nots and alpine sunflowers have some

Specially adapted to withstand harsh climatic conditions above 11,200 feet in elevation, tundra plants endure above Forest Canyon where no trees can survive.
National Park Service

Each spring wild iris paint moist meadows in the park, supplying numerous photo opportunities. Colorful displays of wildflowers advance up the mountains as long summer days continue to warm the earth.

special features, too: Dense hairs reduce heat and water loss and protect them from ultraviolet radiation. The stubby stems and leaves of the sunflower are so hairy that its nickname is old-man-of-the-mountain.

It takes plants hundreds of years to mature in these conditions and decades to recover from damage. Park visitors can help preserve tundra plants by staying on established trails in the three well-marked Tundra Protection Zones off Trail Ridge Road. These paths are a great place to get down on your hands and knees to examine the small-scale world of alpine tundra.

Animals living on tundra have special adaptations, too. White-tailed ptarmigan change colors with the seasons. Camouflaged a mottled brown in summer, the grouselike birds blend in with lichen-covered rocks until snow covers the tundra. By winter, their feathers are pure white, making them nearly impossible to detect. Another year-round resident, the pika, is fun to watch as it works at high speed cutting and drying tundra plants during summer. These little relatives of rabbits store the plants in small haystacks under large rocks. Pikas are active all winter long, living off the stored hay, unlike their waddling neighbors, yellow-bellied marmots. Marmots harvest hay too, but they hibernate in winter. Both of these high elevation characters can communicate to warn of dangers. Listen when you visit the tundra. Pikas call out ear-piercing chirps while marmots send out a variety of high-pitched whistles.

People have been coming to these mountains for more than 10,000 years—but not always on vacation! From the earliest prehistoric hunters to the more recent Arapahos and Utes, humans gathered plants and pursued game for food. Summer was an especially favorite time for the first visitors to be here.

By the 1860s, people began to stay year-round when farmers and ranchers came to Grand Lake and Estes Park. Prospectors added to the population, too, particularly in the upper end of the Kawuneeche Valley, where evidence remains of the brief 1880s mining boom at Lulu City. Few riches were uncovered here though, and the absence of precious metals kept the area from being carved up by mining.

Word spread about the region's great scenery and wildlife. Explorers, adventurers, and business owners followed. One of these newcomers was only 14 when he left his Kansas home in 1884 to live in the Rockies. By 1885, young Enos Mills had climbed Longs Peak and become devoted to these mountains, lakes, and wildlife. He observed nature, writing and sketching and guiding hikers from his guest lodge to the top of Longs Peak. As tourism flourished, Mills joined forces with other early preservationists to promote the idea of a national park. He was passionate when writing and speaking about the natural wonders of his mountain home, and was rewarded in 1915 when Congress established the country's tenth national park.

Naturalist Enos Mills (third from right) shared his passion for these mountains by guiding visitors on hikes to such challenging destinations as Longs Peak.
National Park Service

Visitors stand on the Continental Divide where precipitation'that falls begins a long journey either west to the Gulf of California or east to the Gulf of Mexico. National Park Service

Travel Log

- The west entrance to Rocky Mountain National Park is reached from Grand Lake on U.S. 34. Access from the east is from U.S. 34 west of Loveland or U.S. 36 northwest from Boulder. Colorado 7, the Peak to Peak Scenic and Historic Byway, parallels the eastern boundary of the park, offering great views of Wild Basin and Longs Peak.
- Entrance and camping fees are charged. Five campgrounds accommodate summer park visitors; three campgrounds remain open year-round. Numerous backcountry campsites are available to backpackers.
- Weather can change dramatically at these high elevations (ranging from 7,600 feet near Estes Park to 14,255 feet at the top of Longs Peak). Be aware of dangerous lightning; dress in layers and use sunscreen.

18 The Royal Gorge

Peer through the cracks between the wide weathered boards on the Royal Gorge Bridge and you realize an awesome fact: The planks are the only things between you and the raging Arkansas River, 1,053 feet straight down beneath your shoes!

The highest suspension bridge in the world sways in the wind and bounces slightly as vehicles slowly drive over the same boards that support you. It spans 1,260 feet from canyon rim to rim. Some suspension bridges may be much longer, but no other is as high as the Royal Gorge.

Attracting visitors since 1929, the Royal Gorge Bridge and Cañon City present an interesting mixture of nature and theme park in high desert surroundings. The bridge is the star attraction, but an incline railroad and an aerial tramway owned by Cañon City, are now part of a 5,000-acre park.

The railway, added at the site in 1931, enables visitors to reach the bottom of the canyon and to look up from the banks of the Arkansas River. Built at an angle of 45 degrees, it is the steepest incline railroad in the world, and descends 1,550 feet down Telephone Gulch to the bottom of the canyon. Prior to the incline railroad, only passengers on the Denver & Rio Grande Railroad could look up at the suspension bridge .

In 1969, an aerial tramway was built just east of the bridge. A high-rise ride on the fire-engine red tram provides a silent, gliding flight across the Royal Gorge. This bird's eye view of the suspension bridge can be another highlight of your visit.

Paleo Scene

When you gaze into the gorge from the heights, you may be overwhelmed by geology. Creation of the canyon was the process of landscape uplift and downward cutting by the Arkansas River. What is unusual about the Royal Gorge is that the river carved through solid granite. Researchers estimate that it has taken an average of 2,500 years for each foot, so today's canyon is more than 2.5 million years old! That places its beginnings at about the time of the first dinosaurs.

A man-made connection, the Royal Gorge Bridge crosses the abyss carved by the Arkansas River more than 100 feet below.

Think about those action movies with primitive suspension bridges made from jungle vines or rope. This technique of suspending a walkway or road has been around for hundreds of years and used successfully by many cultures. Suspension bridges are one of the oldest engineering designs employed when the placement of midpoint support piers are impossible to construct. Such bridges often provide an economical way to span a waterway or canyon that otherwise poses a major barrier. How would you construct a bridge over such a gaping canyon? Where would you start? How would the construction of the bridge in 1929 compare to building techniques now?

Building for the Nation

As you walk or drive across the bridge today, it may be easy to dismiss the challenges facing the engineers and construction workers in 1929. Within 10 years of completing the Royal Gorge Bridge, the Empire State Building was built, in 1931; Hoover (Boulder) Dam was completed in 1936; the Golden Gate Bridge in 1937; Mount Rushmore was under construction, too, and finished in 1941.

Lon Piper, a Texan, was in charge of the project, supervising it through to completion. Work began in spring of 1929 and was completed within five

Two steel towers carry the cables to hold the bridge roadway. People, cars, and a tram cross the canyon on wooden planks for a distance of one-quarter mile. Flags from every state line the roadway.

months! Construction started with the concrete bases and steel towers that would eventually hold the large main cables that would, in turn, support the bridge deck from a series of suspender rods.

Once the steel towers were finished, engineers needed to connect the two sides of the canyon. A wire cable was first lowered down each side of the gorge and the two ends of the cable were spliced together and pulled back up. The first cable, called the carry cable, allowed the workers to attach a much thicker wire cable later that would serve as a trolley cable. The trolley cable carried each of the 2,100 wires used for each cable across the canyon. Each suspension cable was 9 inches in diameter, with a 0.75- inch cable core and a bundle of 2,100 wire strands. With so many strong supports, the bridge can hold 2 million pounds, or about 900 pounds per square foot. Check out the section of cable on display in front of the visitor center.

Anchors Away

Crossing over the steel towers on saddle rollers, the cables are anchored into solid rock. Saddle rollers allow for any expansion and contraction of the cables due to temperature changes and wind, eliminating any horizontal stress on the towers that would occur if the cables were permanently attached to the towers.

Once the cables were in place, a specially designed trolley cage was built to ride on the cables. Workers attached collars around the cable and suspended steel rods from the cable collars. The steel bridge frame was then attached to these rods. Wooden planks were laid down and attached to the steel bridge frame. Almost 1,300 wooden planks were needed to create the road surface on the bridge! A fan-shaped array of wires attached to the lower portion of the bridge was added later to minimize swaying in high winds.

Originally, the wire cables were attached to steel pins driven into the solid granite of the canyon wall in an anchor trench. The trench was then filled with concrete and additional steel to strengthen the anchor point.The cable anchoring system was completely refurbished in 1984 after inspections revealed some deterioration. Suspension rods were also replaced with wire rope suspender cables, which are three times stronger than the original rods.

The project was completed in November 1929 and dedicated December 6, less than two months after the stock market crash that started the Great Depression. Most matter-of-fact summaries of the bridge construction don't mention what must have been a significant challenge for the builders of this magnificent bridge. Did these engineers have any doubts about their ability to span the deep canyon? If, during your visit, you can steal a few moments by yourself, try to imagine how you would have approached the job, then and now.

Back in Time Line

Long before the thought of building a bridge across the Royal Gorge occurred, the Grand Canyon of the Arkansas, as it was once called, was at the center of a bitter railroad war. The factions were the Denver & Rio Grande and the Santa Fe Railroads. In 1879 the railroads were racing to claim the canyon as a route to serve mines at the newly discovered silver lode in Leadville, Colorado. There was an armed confrontation at the eastern mouth of the canyon.

Although no shots were fired, plenty of angry words were exchanged between the work crews, along with a lot of high-spirited gun waving. Neither side would back down. During the day, crews laid tracks in different parts of the canyon and dynamited the work of the opposing crews at night! Events became more serious when crews set up barricades and began shooting at each other.They must have been poor marksmen though because no one was killed.

A court decision first awarded the right to use the canyon to the Santa Fe Railroad. This decision was reversed, giving the right to the Denver & Rio Grande Railroad. Confounded, the Santa Fe Railroad hired gunslinger Bat Masterson and his gang to help win back what they thought was theirs. This started another war in which the Denver & Rio Grande Railroad began seizing land from the Santa Fe Railroad. Near the end of December 1879, the court finally issued a settlement that each side could live with. As part of the court decision, the Denver & Rio Grande Railroad was able to complete the tracks through the canyon and on to Leadville.

Because the canyon is so narrow at one point, the railroaders had to build a hanging bridge for the tracks, an ingenious solution for a complicated problem. The hanging bridge is still in place and can be seen from the Royal Gorge Bridge.

At one time, passenger trains with open cars provided visitors to the gorge with spectacular views of the river and the Grand Canyon of the Arkansas. President Theodore Roosevelt visited the beautiful canyon on several occasions. Today, fewer freight and passenger trains use these tracks that shimmer at the bottom of the canyon.

Travel Log

- The Royal Gorge Bridge is about two hours from Denver, west of Cañon City off U.S. 50.The entrance is well-marked. There is an entrance fee and activities depend on the time of the year.
- There is a very nice campground as you approach the Royal Gorge Bridge, and several pullouts for a picnic.
- Whitewater rafting or kayaking through the gorge is rated at class IV or V and guide services do not permit individuals under 16 years of age on these excursions. Contact the Cañon City Chamber of Commerce for rafting information at P.O. Box 749Z, Cañon City, CO 81215; (719) 275-2331 or (800) 876-7922. Other attractions at Cañon City include the Colorado Territorial Prison Museum and Park.

At midpoint, visitors can touch the main cables that support the bridge.
Vibrations from cars and pedestrian traffic can be felt as the bridge bounces
ever so slightly from their passing.

19 San Juan Mountains

"All aboard!"

Black smoke puffs from the stack of the coal-colored steam engine. A crisply dressed conductor shouts the final call for passengers to board the vintage narrow gauge train at the Durango depot. A brakeman makes his final check just as the morning sun spotlights the gold-colored rail cars, one by one. Then, two long whistles pierce the chilly morning air, and the engineer lets the locomotive start to roll. A chug and a clank, and you are on your way to the heart of the San Juan Mountains.

Jeep roads, hiking trails, and scenic byways crisscross this very high region of southwest Colorado, which has more than 5 million acres of magnificent national forests. The Durango & Silverton Narrow Gauge Railroad is its own story: It's the smell of coal smoke, the sound of whistles, and the light touch of ashy cinders landing on your skin that make it such a special trip. Mile by memorable mile, the three-foot-wide track takes you through classic Colorado scenery of stunning mountain meadows, 14,000-foot peaks, cascading waterfalls, old mines, and glimpses of bygone Victorian days.

Hardy adventurers get off at Needleton and cross the Animas River on a footbridge to continue up and up, into the Weminuche Wilderness for a closer view of the wild-looking Needle Mountains. Farther up the tracks, a sign points to the Grenadier Range, slate-gray peaks that invite your eyes up to the sky. Boulders along the river have turned orange from minerals meeting air and water, and mine openings appear high on rocky slopes. After 45 miles of aspens and avalanche chutes, Silverton welcomes passengers to the center of the San Juans.

Savoring the San Juans

• Go on a Sky-High Drive. The 236-mile San Juan Skyway loops through stupendous Colorado scenery. From Ouray to Silverton, you can decide whether there really are flakes of gold in the Million Dollar Highway, or if the scenery simply is worth (at least) a million bucks! In Durango, a town born from the arrival of the railroad in 1880, a flavor of the Old West hitches a ride with visitors all the way to Cortez, Dolores, and Telluride. The beauty of the San Miguel River steers you toward the Dallas Divide which offers an opportunity for some of the best photography in the state on the way to Ridgway.

Durango & Silverton Narrow Gauge Railroad passengers in open cars gaze into the Animas River Gorge.

• Alpine Loop National Backcountry Byway. The side-trip of a lifetime, this 65-mile gravel and dirt road, built in the late 1800s, was designed as a wagon road to cart ore to Silverton, Ouray, and Lake City. Now that most of the mines are inactive, you can tour in four-wheel-drive vehicles, by motorcycle or mountain bikes to wind through seven ghost towns and around five 14,000-foot peaks. Those who brave Cinnamon or Engineer Passes, both over 12,000 feet, from Ouray or Silverton can continue on to Lake San Cristobal, the second largest natural lake in the state.

• No Better Backpacking. Whether you want to scale a fourteener, see the most luscious wildflowers in the state, or hike for miles through alpine meadows, the San Juans are where you must go. When you backpack, the wilderness becomes your domain, and there are five wilderness areas with more lakes and streams than you can count and more peaks than you can name. The San Juan National Forest alone has 500 miles of trails leading to what seems like the top of the world. You may never want to return to civilization.

Paleo Scene

Pausing in the mist on the Box Canyon Boardwalk at Ouray is a lot like standing near trembling train tracks as a locomotive thunders by. Canyon Creek drops 100 feet down a narrow cleft through a smooth limestone grotto here, rumbling endlessly with the awesome power of white and turquoise water plunging over Box Canyon Falls. This place feels like the center of the earth, but the real core of the San Juans lies farther to the south, at Red Mountain Pass.

A blaze of alpine fireweed brightens the roadside along the San Juan Skyway where 236 miles of magnificent mountain views loop around the heart of the San Juans.

Rainbow hues brighten the scenery where the San Juan Skyway crosses a flat valley riddled with mines. You won't wonder how this colorful pass was named—every shade of red from ruby to rust tints surface soils where iron-bearing minerals have combined with oxygen. In some places, the fiery-colored ground offers prospectors and geologists clues about more valuable minerals concealed nearby. Over the years, gold, lead, zinc, and silver have been mined out of these mountains in unmatched amounts.

Why is this region so rich in minerals? At Red Mountain Pass, visitors enter the Silverton caldera, a collapsed ancient volcano. Millions of years ago, one huge mountain groaned and shook here, faults formed in a circular pattern, and the summit slid into empty magma chambers. Igneous rocks produced from volcanic heat filled up every crack, fissure, and fault of the Silverton caldera. Within these crevices, some thousands of feet deep and many miles wide, lie veins of wealth that have produced millions and millions of dollars in silver and gold alone. Glaciers later scoured out U-shaped valleys and high mountain cirques from the caldera, wiping out the most obvious evidence of its volcanic beginnings.

Crypto Scene

You may not know you are a train fan until you arrive in Durango. Amos Cordova, who is with the Durango & Silverton Narrow Gauge Railroad, says, "Everyone has a little railroad blood, and it always comes out when you hear the whistle blow."

It seems trains can talk, from clickty-clack, to whistles, chugs, chuffs, and clanks. Engineers and firemen even feel locomotives have their own personality, whistle, and character. Listen to the language of the steam-driven engines as they carry passengers between Durango and Silverton. The engineer uses the shrill whistle to communicate specific messages to the crew.

Whether you are riding the train along the Animas River or strolling around the town of Silverton, it's fun to know the universal train language and understand how the crew communicates. These are some of the locomotive sounds you may hear along the railroad. Each • stands for a short whistle and each — indicates a long whistle.

—	Approaching station or junction.
•	Apply brakes. Stop.
— —	Release brakes. Proceed.
• •	Proceed through station or junction.
• • •	Stop at station or junction.
— — • —	Approaching public road crossings at grade.
— — •	Approaching point to meet or wait for other trains.
— • • •	Flagman protect rear of train.
• • • —	Flagman protect front of train.

There are even more combinations to learn, but these are a few that will have you understanding train language right away.

Wild Things

Imagine how the San Juan Mountains must have swarmed with wildlife before miners and railroaders arrived. Mountain goats, bighorn sheep, black bear, cougar, and deer probably inhabited every corner of this wild region. More than a century of human impact has passed, but hikers and backcountry travelers continue to encounter herds of skittish elk and plenty of signs of beaver. There is one mysterious character in this wildlife drama that stumps biologists.

Could grizzly bears still roam the wild San Juans? Recent signs and sightings suggest that these mountain monarchs might still live in a portion of their historic habitat. The animals were thought to have been hunted to extinction by ranchers and government trappers, but research reveals that a handful of native Colorado grizzlies could actually be hiding out like outlaws in the southern San Juans today.

What is so important about a few rambling bears? Native grizzlies enduring decades of human activity testify to the vast wildness of the San Juan Mountains. Such survivors add real richness to the region, too. Suppose you were certain that grizzly bears were gone from the San Juans forever. Wouldn't something be missing from the scenery? How would a grizzly make your trip different?

Micro Scape

Each fall, an artist's palette of salmon, gold, orange, yellow, and green paints the San Juans where aspen cloak the mountainsides. What causes bright green aspen leaves to turn such vivid colors in autumn? As days grow shorter and nights grow longer, a chemical clock inside each tree starts ticking. As time passes, a substance released inside each aspen cuts off the flow of sap to the leaves. Within each leaf, pigments such as chlorophyll give plants their color and enable them to convert sunlight to food energy. Chlorophyll absorbs reds and blues from sunlight, reflecting only green. As fall advances, the reduced sap flow decreases the amount of chlorophyll, and the green leaves no longer supply the plant with energy. Leftover sap concentrates as it dries up, allowing the reds, oranges, and yellows of fall to take over. The intensity of fall color depends upon seasonal factors such as drought, rain, snow, and cold. Great autumn aspen displays usually result from dry, sunny days and crisp, chilly nights.

Back in Time Line

In 1860, a year before Colorado Territory was created, the discovery of gold in these mountains brought a rush of miners, and then the railroads, wagon roads, and towns that you see in the San Juans today. Before the gold rush the San Juans had been used as a tribal hunting ground by the Ute Indians for hundreds of years. Consider what life must have been like for the 3,000 Utes

Ouray's colorful Victorian buildings hug the base of an enormous rock amphitheater like jewels in the bottom of a big bowl. This picturesque mountain hamlet, dotted by cascading waterfalls and soothing hot springs, was named for the Ute chief who shared his people's mountain home with miners and settlers. Chief Ouray and his tribe were rewarded only with exile to reservations outside the San Juans.

living there: fishing and hunting in the big amphitheaters of the San Juans; visiting sacred hot springs; growing up healthy and free with clean air and water all around. This is how Chief Ouray and his wife, Chipeta, existed among their Ute neighbors—before stories of mineral wealth in the west pushed territorial officials to try and remove them from the mountains and open up land for mining.

The Rush Was On

In 1860, news of a gold rush along the Animas River attracted hundreds of miners to Baker's Park. But the Civil War (1860–1865), winter snows, and angry Ute Indians who resented trespassing prospectors delayed mining. In 1868, the United States government established a Ute reservation that included the San Juans, and promised the Utes that the land would be theirs "as long as the grasses grow and the waters flow." The treaty did not allow settlers, miners, or anyone else to trespass on Ute lands.

Prospectors ignored the treaty; the lure of silver and gold was too much. The Utes protested, President Ulysses Grant ordered troops to defend Ute territory, but Colorado officials withdrew the action, informing Washington leaders that discussions with the Utes would eventually lead to their surrender.

At the same time, road-builder Otto Mears was grading trails into the San Juans to supply miners and carry out mineral-rich ore. Mears became acquainted with Ute Chief Ouray, who was recognized by the U.S. government as spokesman for the Ute Indians. In 1873, when another attempt at a treaty with the Utes failed, Mears was invited to assist with negotiations. As a result,

Chief Ouray agreed to give 4 million acres of the San Juan mountain tops to the United States.

Miners greedily took over the fertile valley bottoms as well. Ore hauled out by the ton from Baker's Park gave the booming town its new name: Silverton. Telluride, Rico, and Placerville sprang up overnight, creating a demand for transportation and services that would soon seal the fate of the Utes. Although the lovely Victorian town of Ouray was named in honor of the cooperative Ute chief, all of his people were exiled to reservations south of the San Juans and west to Utah by 1881.

From Trails to Rails

Otto Mears remained, connecting Placerville, Telluride, and Ophir with a toll road and working on his most famous project, the Million Dollar Highway. One story suggests that the gravel surface of this road contained $1 million in gold! The real gold, though, was probably found at the Bear Creek Falls toll gate, where a $5 fee was collected from each horse-drawn wagon carting ore or carrying supplies.

Mears greatest notion, and the one that made him the richest, was to bring the Denver & Rio Grande Railway to Colorado's mining country. By 1881, tracks stretched from Denver to Durango, and on to Silverton by 1882. By the time the Sherman Silver Purchasing Act was passed, which provided for

Hundreds of miles of trails and five wilderness areas make the San Juan Mountains a backpacker's paradise, but hikers must prepare for frequent rains that keep mountain meadows green all summer long.

the purchase of all the silver produced in the nation at the going price, the new Rio Grande Southern Railroad connected Durango to Telluride and Ridgway.

Silver practically poured out of the mountains once the railroad was completed so that it could be carried out quickly and inexpensively. The railroad also carried livestock and crops to market from ranches near Dolores and along the Dallas Divide.

Mears had one dream left: to connect Silverton to Ouray by rail. Unfortunately, political events interrupted his hopes when the Sherman Silver Purchasing Act was repealed in 1893, and the price of the sterling metal plunged overnight.The San Juan mining boom slowed; miners turned to gold for their livelihoods.

You still sense railroad and mining history everywhere you go in the San Juans. On the Alpine Loop from Lake City over Engineer Pass, you can almost see the ghosts of bearded prospectors piling up bags of ore to haul over one of Otto Mears' toll roads. Between Dolores and Placerville, on the San Juan Skyway, you can practically hear an engine strain on the grade toward the Wilson Mountains and Lizard Head Pass.

A lot less imagination is required on the Durango & Silverton Narrow Gauge Railroad, though. When the creaking train with its gold cars sneaks along the edge of the Animas Gorge past countless avalanche chutes and chugs into Silverton Depot, you almost expect to be greeted by miners and mules. Here, the past is the present, and not a single day of the last century seems to have gone by.

Travel Log

- The San Juans occupy much of the region between Cortez and Durango to the south and Ridgway and Lake City to the north. From Montrose or Durango, U.S. 550 goes to Ouray and Silverton. From Cortez, Colorado 45 takes travelers from Dolores to Telluride. U.S 160 climbs Wolf Creek Pass in the east, to Pagosa Springs and Durango.
- Lodging is available in towns throughout the region. There are hot springs in Ouray, Pagosa Springs, and at Trimble Hot Springs. Camping, hiking, fishing, and mountain biking information is available from San Juan National Forest, 701 Camino Del Rio, Durango, CO 81301, (970) 247-4874; Rio Grande National Forest, 1803 W. Hwy. 160, Monte Vista, CO, 81144, (719) 852-5941; Uncompahgre National Forest, 2250 Hwy. 50, Delta, CO 81416; (970) 874-7691.
- Reservations for the Durango & Silverton Narrow Gauge Railroad can be made by calling (970) 247-2733. Round-trip train rides make for a very full day, so if your time is limited, you may want to consider shuttling or taking a bus in one direction. Cinders can get into your eyes, so wear glasses for a more comfortable excursion. Trains run from the Durango depot year-round, with shorter, winter trips.

20
United States Air Force Academy

Discovery Zone

A spirited crowd roars its approval as a falcon, mascot of the U.S. Air Force Academy, swoops and spirals above Falcon Stadium during the annual football game with rival U.S. Naval Academy midshipmen.

Falcon mascots provide much more than just halftime interest, though. These trained birds of prey have attributes that represent the school's commitment to excellence and the role the Air Force plays in protecting our nation. Attending a football game is a lot of fun, but it disguises the serious business of training students to assume leadership roles. Explore the academy beyond sports, and you will glimpse cadet life and the training program of the United States Air Force.

What's it like to be an Air Force cadet at one of the finest colleges in the nation? What are the pillars of their four-year program? Meet two cadets and explore the campus of this exceptional college to understand how the academy achieves such distinction.

Back to School Time

Established in 1954, this federally funded, national institution just north of Colorado Springs graces 18,000 acres of a former ranch in the foothills of the Rockies. It is a busy college campus where the mission, similar to the U.S. Military Academy and the U.S. Naval Academy, is to educate cadets to serve as officers in the U.S. Air Force, as pilots and civil engineers and in security forces and communications. There are many training activities not open to the public, but some buildings are open to all.

At noon, in the quadrangle, visitors may see long lines of men and women in uniforms standing straight and tall as they prepare to march to lunch. This is the noon formation. Another impressive formation is late afternoon during the retreat ceremony when the United States flag is lowered at the end of the day. If an Air Force aircraft is nearby during a retreat, the pilot is invited to pay a courtesy call, with a low altitude fly-over of the quadrangle. Such a spectacle is an unforgettable bonus.

A marble marker on the quadrangle quotes a portion of the creed that guides these leaders of tomorrow: "Man's flight through life is sustained by the power of his knowledge." Such a philosophy promotes outstanding academy graduates.

Towed aloft by its tow plane, a glider crosses in front of Pikes Peak. Air Force cadets look forward to riding the thermal lifts along the Front Range, with only the rushing wind to propel them.

Crypto Scene

Secrets can be ideas and ideals. There is an atmosphere of excellence at the U.S. Air Force Academy. The Cadet Honor Code exemplifies the academy's commitment to values such as honesty: Cadets pledge to, "not lie, steal or cheat, nor tolerate among us anyone who does."

Fulfilling Your Dream

Such commitment to excellence and success begins very early for some cadets. Rochelle Ng-A-Qui, from Parker, Colorado, is one of about 600 female cadets at the school, or 15 percent of the student body. Rochelle decided to attend the Air Force Academy when she was in the fourth grade and took steps to accomplish her dream by joining the Civil Air Patrol in the ninth grade and learned to fly during high school. She is determined to become a fighter pilot. Rochelle thinks it is important to be involved in a variety of activities while in junior high and high school, and to pursue your dream. "You can only help others," she says, "if you have helped yourself reach your own goals in life."

About 9,000 men and women apply to the U.S. Air Force Academy each year and about 2,000 are accepted, of whom 89 percent are in the top fifth

Pilots in training advance through a series of aircraft as they earn their wings. This airplane is a propeller drive T-3. The student and the instructor sit side by side in the cockpit. U.S. Air Force Academy

of their high school class. Once enrolled, cadets concentrate on developing physically, professionally, intellectually, and in character: the four pillars of excellence.

Cadets are constantly on the go. They learn how to parachute, pilot a glider, navigate, and receive orientation as pilots. Students make 17 glider flights and may practice aerobatic maneuvers after their twelfth flight. They also receive specialized training called survival, evasion, resistance, and escape (SERE), a 20-day course to learn techniques and how to use equipment to increase their chances of survival should they find themselves in enemy territory. There are classroom sessions and seven days in the mountains to learn how to evade capture and, if imprisoned, how to survive and how to help search aircraft locate them for rescue.

After four years at the academy, cadets receive a bachelor of science degree and are commissioned second lieutenants in the Air Force. As new officers they assume a variety of responsibilities, and only a few become pilots.

Wild Things

Added to the thrill of watching an academy football game is to see a prairie falcon perform at speeds approaching 100 miles an hour. The more you learn about the U.S. Air Force Academy, the more you understand why a falcon was chosen as its mascot.

Symbol of the Academy

The first class to enter the Air Force Academy, in 1954, selected the falcon for its courage, speed, keen eyesight, alertness, and powerful flight—all traits that the cadets felt characterized the combat role of the U.S. Air Force. Since then cadets have spent huge amounts of time caring for and training their mascots.

Freshmen are encouraged to become involved in extracurricular activities. During the second semester, upper class members of the falconry club invite freshmen to the falcon enclosures, or mews, to meet the regal birds of prey. Carl Haney, from Chatham, Illinois, an upper classman, said that 56 cadets responded to the invitation one year, but only 16 cadets took the Colorado Division of Wildlife's raptor licensing examination. Cadets who pass the exam earn a license as a certified falconer, and only four are picked to represent their class. Once selected, they are allowed to wear a distinctive patch on the right shoulder of their lightweight jackets.

Caring for the falcons is like having a full-time job while attending school. Falconry is a time-consuming activity: Training a new bird requires 300 hours of work, and daily chores include cleaning the enclosures, feeding the falcons, and raising quails, the primary food for the falcons. Male (tiercels) and female (falcons) are used in the program and usually there are 12 birds at any one time.

Training involves flying a falcon tied to a creance, or long line, at greater and greater distances until the day the creance can be removed and replaced

Cadet falconer Carl Haney holds a gyrfalcon, the official mascot of the Air Force Academy. One of 12 cadet falconers who tend to the academy mascots, Haney devotes many long hours to their care and enjoys the chance to work with these magnificent birds of prey.

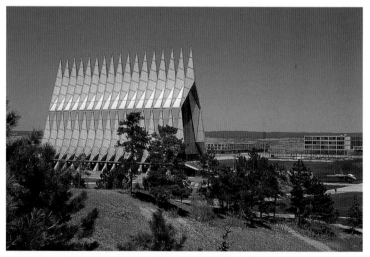

No other building is more closely identified with the Air Force Academy than the Cadet Chapel. Its soaring spires and stained glass interior form a distinctive architectural landmark on the campus.

with a tiny radio transmitter. The falcon, rather than taking food from the hand of the cadet, flies to a lure, a small leather pouch with a piece of meat attached to it.The bird is allowed to hit the lure several times to ensure success at getting the food. Then, after a falcon circles the area to gain altitude, the falconer swings the lure high to attract the bird's attention. The falcon dives at the lure, but the cadet pulls it away at the last second. The falcon tries again, circling to dive a second time. Each session builds the bird's stamina, and training must be very carefully done to keep from discouraging the falcon, causing it to fly away.

It's not all hard work and no fun for cadet falconers. Flying the birds at sporting events is just one of the rewards for hard work. Can you imagine how nervous you might be as a cadet flying a falcon at a football game for the first time? The falcons are taken to many school programs and other public events—an average of 270 each year. They even fly—in an airplane—to away football games. During flights, birds sit on the gloved hand of the falconers. Each falcon usually has a leather hood over its head so it won't be distracted by surrounding activities.

Carl enjoys being able to talk with people and confesses that he is sometimes a little shy, but that it is a lot easier to talk with such a magnificent bird on his hand.

Micro Scape

The most popular destination for visitors is the Cadet Chapel; it can be seen from Interstate 25, but the beauty of this landmark can be appreciated only up close. The chapel is open daily, but may be closed for special events such as weddings and funerals.

The chapel's glowing stained glass windows are set in soaring walls. Each major denomination has a chapel, and there is an All-Faiths Room so that other religious groups have a place for worship.

Travel Log

• The U.S. Air Force Academy is just north of Colorado Springs on Interstate 25. The exits are well marked and directions to the Barry Goldwater Visitor Center are posted at intersections on the grounds. Self-guiding tours are an enjoyable way to experience the academy at a leisurely pace.

• The visitor center displays exhibits on cadet dorm rooms, portions of the training program, and shows a film about the cadet training experience. There is also a gift store and restaurant. The visitor center is open daily 9 a.m. to 5 p.m., and until 6 p.m. in summer. It's closed Thanksgiving, Christmas, and New Year's.

Additional Reading

All adventures start with research: maps, books, pamphlets, and articles. The administrators of most sites in the book and local Chambers of Commerce have compiled useful brochures and pamphlets that are readily available at the scene or by mail. Most federal agencies have compiled informative maps. It's worth calling or writing before you head out for a day, a weekend, or a week. The authors recommend the following sources for a start.

The Air Force Academy Candidate Book. William L. Smallwood, Beacon Books, Buhl, Idaho, 1995.

The Black Canyon. Rose Houk, Southwest Parks and Monument Association, Tucson, Arizona, 1991.

Cinders and Smoke. Doris Osterwald, Western Guideways, Ltd., Lakewood, Colorado, 1995.

Colorado Atlas & Gazetteer. DeLorme Mapping, Freeport, Maine, 1991.

Dinosaur Lake. Martin Lockley, Colorado Geological Survey, Denver, Colorado, 1997.

From Grassland to Glacier: The Natural History of Colorado and the Surrounding Region. Cornelia Fleischer Mutel and John C. Emerick, Johnson Printing, Boulder, Colorado, 1992

Great Sand Dunes, the Shape of the Wind. Stephen Trimble, Southwest Parks and Monuments Association, Tucson, Arizona, 1990.

Marble: A Town Built On Dreams. Oscar McCollum Jr., Sundance Publications, Denver, Colorado, 1992.

Marble, Colorado: City of Stone. Duane Vandenbusche and Rex Myers, Golden Bell Press, Denver, Colorado 1970.

Mesa Verde, The Story Behind the Scenery. Linda Martin, KC Publications, Las Vegas, Nevada, 1993.

Rim of Time: The Canyons of Colorado National Monument. Stephen Trimble, Colorado National Monument Association, Fruita, Colorado, 1993.

Roadside Geology of Colorado. Halka Chronic, Mountain Press Publishing, Missoula, Montana, 1980.

Rocky Mountain National Park: A History. C. W. Buchholtz, Colorado Associated University Press, Niwot, Colorado, 1983.

The Shortgrass Prairie. Ruth Carol Cushman and Stephen R. Jones, Pruett Publishing, Boulder, Colorado, 1988.

Tracking Dinosaurs: A New Look at the Ancient World. Martin Lockley, Cambridge University Press, Cambridge, England, 1991.

The Authors

Diane T. Liggett and James A. Mack share a strong interest in authentic destinations as well as preservation of natural and cultural resources. National Park Service employees, the authors combine more than 30 years of natural history education and editorial experience, with numerous awards for development of special interpretive programs and publications. Diane received a Bachelor of Science Degree in Botany from California State Polytechnic

University and currently develops educational publications and exhibits. Jim holds a Bachelor of Science Degree in Wildlife Biology from California State University and is Superintendent of Fort Laramie National Historic Site in Wyoming.